Spiritual Journey

How To Get Through The Day

by Elizabeth Kelly

Library of Congress Catalog Card Number 97-68218

ISBN 0-9659075-0-3

Published by CIMARRON BOOKS, P. O. Box 808, Yellow Springs, Ohio 45387-0808.   Fax (937) 767-1499

Photograph of Elizabeth Kelly by Theresa Thinnes & David Willis, *Dancing Light Photography Studio & Gallery*, Yellow Springs, Ohio.

For the availability of autographed copies of this book, contact:
EPIC BOOK SHOP
118 Dayton Street
Yellow Springs, OH 45387
(937) 767-7997

This book is dedicated to Hap Cawood and his wife, Sonia, and their daughters Romy and Shuly. Without their perseverance, patience and sympathy, there would be no book.
— *E.K.*

Table of Contents

Chapter 1 — You have vast hidden resources

You are what you believe 1
We are co-creators 5
Bank on group energy 8
You have the philosopher's stone 10
We are all one 11
Convert the energy 14
Think what you want to become 15
Choose 16
Life goes on; we go on with it 18
What you give, you get 20
Life is a school 23

Chapter 2 — You are more than the body

See people as energy 29
Change the vibration 32
Knowledge we acquire; truth we realize 34
Death isn't all that much 34

Chapter 3 — Change yourself

Be critical within 37
Others must ask 42
Choose not to suffer 43
Love one another 48
Make up your mind to be happy 53

Look beyond your little melodrama 55
Don't judge others 58
Don't have expectations 60
Exemplify what you believe 62
Live courageously 64
Do it yourself 68
Nowhere is someplace 69
Love yourselves, too 71
Cherish your time 72
Be aware 73
Once aware, you cannot be lonely 75
No one owns another 76
Silently absorb the qualities of others 77
You are like your friends 78
Bless others 79
Be more 79
Angry people speak to themselves 80
Good is a matter of direction 81
Serve 82
Don't be a doormat 84
Don't accept anything resentfully 84
Love must evolve 85
Miracles are everyday 87
Be grateful 89
Stay in the moment 90
To have more, want less 90
Keep learning 91
Do the divine duty before you 91

Chapter 4 — Techniques for strength

Learn to be artists in religion 93
Love God your way 96
Find freedom in discipline 97
Pray 99
Practice the presence of God 100
Evaluate your day 101
Use inner problem-solving methods 102
Repeat an affirmation 106
Use symbols 108
Meditate 109

Chapter 5 — I promise you: a conversation

. . . . 113

Poems

Truth 27
The Mind 31
Death 36
Dream's End 58
Disaster 67
Time 74
Horses 98
Mistaken 111
Now 127

ELIZABETH KELLY

Introduction

BORN August 12, 1912 in St. Louis, Missouri, Elizabeth Louise Tubbs married Robert Kelly in 1934. In 1963 they settled in Yellow Springs, Ohio. She dedicated the middle years of her life to her family and to bringing up her four sons, while pursuing artistic and civic interests. Though intuitively gifted from an early age, she spoke little of her unusual experiences when she was young.

In the early 1970s, people began coming to her for counsel. By 1975, her compassion and insight were attracting crowds to informal weekly talks. Several dozen of those talks were recorded by friends. Transcribed, they were edited into the first version of this book, which also included some of her poems. The book was revised and slightly expanded for this small-format edition.

Elizabeth Kelly reverently regards the saints of all religions. She counts as a spiritual highlight of her life a 1928 meeting with Paramahansa Yogananda, author of the spiritual classic, *Autobiography of a Yogi*, a work she has often recommended.

You have vast hidden resources

1. You are what you believe

IF YOU ASK PEOPLE if they believe in God, they will say, "Yes, I believe in God." But if you know them, you will see that they believe in liquor or sex or drugs or hard work or money — a million things — but not God.

Our belief is demonstrated by what we depend on. Our lives are our religions. If we believe in things that are vulnerable, then we take on that same vulnerability.

You are all fortunate to be in a physical body. The physical dimension offers the means by which you can test your beliefs. Because you had certain beliefs and desires, you were brought into the body to test them. Otherwise, you would be floating around in space as an idea.

Do you believe in love? Here you can prove it.

Do you believe money is what makes you happy? Here you can learn.

We are all going through a continual testing of what we

really believe and know. Consequently, we must realize that there are no idle moments. There is no idle speech. There are no idle thoughts. All thoughts and words have power.

As part of your test, you will meet people who are vital to you. The people you know well are those you have known in other lives. You are brought together as a blessing or to learn some lesson. We travel in and out of this Earth in shoals, like fish. We are divine fellow-travelers. We go, shoal-like, to God.

The purpose of your own life is to find the God out of Whom you came, as a wave comes out of the ocean. You have always existed. You may think that you are your body, your ego. You are not. You are more, more than you can imagine.

God is the source of all creation, in whom all creation is, just as the dreamer is the dreamer, the dream and the objects of the dream. Once we wake up, we know that we are part of the dreamer.

We wake up by regaining our God-consciousness. This is the basis of all great religions. Regaining this consciousness is the universal religion.

BY LOVING God we activate the very spirit of God within. Just as we descended from God, we must ascend again. The first step of our return is to expand our consciousness. That expansion comes through love.

As we expand our love and awareness, we expand our joy. This is all the more vital because the world is entering a new age, and the transition will be difficult and long. The more you flow with life and the truth, the more control you will have.

If you learn to see God in all others, in all things and in yourself, you link yourself to a transcendent power. You become harmless to yourself and others.

One of the great achievements of life is to become harmless. Few realize how difficult, how blessed that triumph is.

I AM NOT REALLY TELLING YOU something you don't already know. Deep inside, you know the truth. Truth is not something manufactured by people. It exists.

You must think of yourself and others as icebergs. The physical body and the conscious mind are the visible part. But the hidden part is gigantic. It contains records of accomplishment and error, patterns of mistakes and powers of the soul.

When you learn that this soul power is there, and that it responds to your plea for enlightenment and guidance, you begin to become aware. That awareness can be developed by meditation and regular periods of prayer.

The hidden part of the iceberg is the part of the mind beyond the conscious level. Developing knowledge of this is the major contribution to science and mankind by such great psychiatrists as Sigmund Freud and Carl Jung.

THE TRIUNE NATURE of reality and God is accounted for and described many ways in science and religion as:

Causal, astral and physical;

Ideas, energy and matter;

Father, Son and the Holy Spirit, which the Hindus call Sat, Tat and Aum.

As microcosms of the triune creation, we, too, exist as spiritual, mental and physical levels. Some of these levels are hidden from us.

Long ago we descended into physical creation. We became enamored of living at the physical level and forgot our true nature and origin. Enticed by the apple of sensual knowledge in the midst of the nerve tree within, we fell from Eden.

Fortunately, we can go back. The Bible tells us this. The Bhagavad-Gita tells us this. The Buddha tells us this.

In that journey back, we can use the knowledge to become happier here, now, as we are.

It matters more that we love God than that we call God by any particular name — Heavenly Father, Divine Mother, Jehovah, Allah, Great Spirit, Oversoul. God has many aspects to help us personalize the impersonal, but names of the One should not divide us.

We are parts of God. And the whole is greater than the sum of its parts.

2. We are co-creators

WE ARE CO-CREATORS of the future with God. Because God is in all of you, you can create anything you want, have anything you want. In the fullness of time, you will get whatever you want badly enough. This is not really the difficulty. The difficulty is learning what you really want, learning what really makes you happy.

Remember always that desire is a force so strong it can survive even your physical body. Desire is the force by which you brought yourself into the body and to the circumstances around you.

Thoughts are things. If you can believe it, know that thoughts are more permanent than matter. Desire is one of the strongest thoughts. Be careful how you use it. When you use desire to know God, when your desire and persistence are fired by divine love, you will come to know God.

ALL THE TIME MY CHILDREN WERE GROWING UP, I would say to them, "Be careful what you wish. You are likely to get it. Don't be casual. Don't be casual. Be aware. Be responsible. Love God."

Once you realize that this is God's world and that He runs it, and that your own spirit comes from God, you realize you are a co-creator.

Once you overcome your petty desires and attachments, you are guided by your higher Self.

You are no longer carried here and there by petty wants and fantasies.

You begin to walk by the light that is within you.

You realize that you can make life whatever you want it to be.

SOME PEOPLE realize their creative potential without knowing about God. They don't go to church. It doesn't concern me. I have dear friends who are absolutely devoted atheists, but their lives are virtuous and purposeful. Even if they don't say to God, "I love you," God's world continues right along. But if they realized the force of which they are a part, it would give them more depth, grace and understanding. It would open the inner world and give proof to them.

We will explore that inner world just as Christopher Columbus and Admiral Byrd explored the outer world. It is just as exciting and much more vast. In the various dimensions of your reality you may meet things that terrify you and things you will love, and they will transform your whole conception of the universe.

You can do it yourself, wherever you are. And it isn't going to cost you anything.

WE ARE NOT HERE AS HELPLESS VICTIMS. We are bound only by our own ignorance. All you have to do is open your heart. If you can turn from the world and in your true heart say, "There is nothing here; there is only God," then you will see that God is in everyone. You will see God.

The physical level is one of duality, of opposites — of man and woman, negative and positive, birth and death, heat and cold, yin and yang. However, that is not the way reality is at the finer levels. From these levels your soul leaks to your conscious mind the kind of awareness you call extrasensory perception.

The law of cause and effect works in all dimensions. For every physical action there is an equal reaction. For every spiritual action there is a reaction. Eastern religions call the reaction karma. Western religions refer to the creation of negative karma as sin.

The law holds that whatever you do to others will be done to you. That law operates precisely because we are all one. It teaches us — no matter how long it takes us to learn — that we are inseparable.

Some might ask: What happens to the person who kills others in anger, yet he dies of natural causes? We haven't developed the consciousness to see the law work in its full measure. Dear ones, the killer will live the misery he caused — but perhaps in subsequent lifetimes.

The terror of life is not in its apparent unfairness but in its order.

It is not God who causes us misery, for God is love. Misery is what we have made of our God-given free will, acting within the law of cause and effect. The law's purpose is to teach us to rise above our painful ignorance. Ignorance is the notion of separateness from God. Sin is whatever increases that separation.

3. Bank on group energy

SINCE YOUR physical, mental and spiritual habits set up an energy pattern, it is helpful to gather in a group and turn your thoughts to God. By doing that, you benefit from the energy that is around you. When you gather to concentrate on God, you help set up a vibration that is good not only for the moment but is also useful for your future.

Throughout the week, if you are tired or need something to sustain you, you have only to remember the gathering and the peace of the group experience, and this energy will flow through you.

People in loving groups, where the essence is prayer or devotion or meditation, develop an energy that is very much like an entity. It might help to think of it as a genie. You can call on this energy for help. If you are tired, try to visualize the energy, and it will reinforce you.

Actually it is an expansion of your own energy and your own consciousness. Often it is difficult for us to realize these potentials are within us; thus it helps to visualize them outwardly.

Remember, *anything you can recognize, you can use.* That does not mean you should get caught up in powers and abilities that divert you from the quest for God-awareness.

When you advance spiritually, you may contact energies that you should not deal with. That is why I ask you not to do automatic writing or use the Ouija board. These are channels of energy that have nothing to do with the quest for God. You do not have enough control over these energies; they can easily gain control over you.

Anchor yourself simply to the search for God, aware that human beings — all of you — are very much like atomic bombs, with enormous power.

You have to know how to use that energy.

You have to especially know how not to use it and why you should not get caught up in the glamour of power and submission to forces that do not reflect the divine will.

4. You have the philosopher's stone

IF YOU CONTEMPLATE GOD in meditation, the mind expands itself. The realization of God is a non-verbal experience. When you reach the finer states of mind, you will know that you have reached them. There will be no question. You will see the light, hear the Amen [Aum], know the spirit behind all things, merge with all.

The main goal is to make yourself what the Hindus call "one-pointed." Kirkegaard explained it as the purity of heart "to will one thing."

Simply put, the key is this:

The conscious mind reasons.

The subconscious mind remembers and imagines.

The superconscious mind realizes.

If you use the conscious mind to reach the other levels by thinking of God, remembering God, and realizing that it is God's world — if you can hold to this thought day after day, and do what you have to do as well as you can, I promise you that your lives will be transformed.

It is simple. So simple.

We make life a fantasy of hobgoblins and agonies and one thing or another.

Give them up.

Anchor yourself to God.

If you can master the idea of the conscious mind reasoning, the subconscious mind remembering and the superconscious mind realizing, and the laser-like power of focusing these three levels on God, you will come to know the basis of the miraculous happenings that emerge from the divinity within you, which come from the source of divinity Itself.

By opening your mind to its levels, you will see reality at its levels. At the ordinary conscious level, you see matter as matter. At the superconscious levels, you next see matter as light and energy, and then you see the energy and matter as creative ideas of God. When you realize the world as ideas, you see how, as a child of God, your ideas can create.

This is the philosopher's stone.

5. We are all one

AT THE HIGHEST states of consciousness, we realize our oneness. Then it is beyond argument.

Until we reach that state, we must reason that we are one. It is an ethic that works, but it is true beyond its ethical utility.

There are no insignificant lives. All lives are equal. If we believe there is a fundamental difference between the great scientist and the retarded child, we are not seeing people as they really are. We are seeing the tip of the iceberg and neglecting the vast soul beneath.

Some people say, "If we could just get rid of the misfits, everything would be all right." I know from my own experience that some persons you might regard as misfits or retarded or odd are here for the enlightenment and advancement of those they meet. They are here at enormous sacrifice.

WE FLOW THROUGH one another's bloodstreams and we see through one another's eyes. We are all locked into a matrix we think is circumstance, in a precise calculus of time. There is no way we can be separate.

When we realize that we all are one, we won't have wars. We won't have depressions. We won't have such great difficulties. We certainly will not live in the way we live now. The way we live now is unbelievable, it is so barbaric.

In the future, we will live in functioning communities, aware of how ridiculous it is to separate people by ages — teenagers here, oldsters there.

We are all one.

We learn from one another.

We understand from one another.

OUR MENTAL, PHYSICAL AND SPIRITUAL HABITS make a box, and we stay in that box. The box is built of preconceived notions of how the world is and how we should be treated. It is very limiting.

The only way to escape the box is to come to the realization of oneness.

I have a Sudanese friend, a Moslem, who never takes a drink without spilling a few drops for those who are dying of thirst in the desert. The awareness of these things acknowledges our unity and prevents us from having to live through suffering to attain sensitivity.

LISTEN TO EVERYONE. Realize God is in everyone. Love the God in them, and don't get hung up on the rest. Sometimes we love people because they look like this or that or because they flatter us. To the extent that we gain pleasure from such superficial appreciation, we will suffer pain, because the things we think are important are not.

The true sin is to believe we are separate.

Being inseperable in essence, all lives are significant. No matter what we do, in essence we cannot become less. We can realize more of what we are. Or we can shut ourselves off from our souls and think we are less.

But at the finer levels of our being, we are points of light, pulsating in God.

(Pulse is very important. If you are in difficulty, or are lonely, and it seems difficult to anchor yourself in God, you

can be comforted by a clock or something that pulsates.
The attraction is universal.)

As little dots of light, we are aware of compassion, love
and kindness, but we cannot exemplify them. Here, on the
physical plane, we can exemplify what we believe.

Here we can test ourselves to see what we really
believe. The sole purpose of our being here is to realize
our true nature, the God within us.

You can experience God.

Anybody can do it.

But we spend our time working, sleeping, playing,
eating — and we do not spend much time trying to realize
God.

6. Convert the energy

ALL EMOTION that becomes contained can become
dangerous. We should all constantly realize that energy
flows through us. Our task is to refine and direct it. Love
flows through. Hatred flows through. The more we can
generate love and transform the energy into love, the more
it replaces the other debilitating energies.

There are ways to use the energy that surrounds us in
nature. This understanding eventually will enable the
world to increase its food supply as the Earth changes.

Though physical resources and nutrients seem limited, the energy surrounding us is limitless.

If you do not direct your energies toward God, you still are just as much a part of God. But you are locked into a time-space. You will stay there until you suffer enough at this level and become humble enough to turn toward the source of your own life and freedom.

7. Think what you want to become

THE MIND is like a sheet of water, formless. It will reflect anything. It will absorb anything that you place before it.

So if you constantly think "My health is very poor," or, "Alas, it is a terrible thing to get old," or, "Whatever will become of us?" — then disaster is going to overcome you as soon as you can pull it in the door. The mind absorbs these notions; the absorption makes them real, and they come back to us over and over again. So think of God to find God.

Your ability to find God has nothing to do with life after death or what day you are going to eat or whether you missed Sunday School. It has nothing to do with any kind of doctrine. Your ability to find God has only to do with the reality of the world and what you want to know and become.

8. Choose

PLANTS ARE AWARE at a certain level, but they do not suffer, for their level of pain is not as high as in animals. Plants and animals are naturally evolving to God.

Human beings are more aware, self-aware. Consequently, you can choose.

If you were compelled to go to God, you would be God's slave, not one made in His image. You would not be a part of God. But being part of God, you are able to choose.

WHAT YOU DO AND THINK in one life determines what you will be in subsequent ones. You are, in this life, the sum of what you have made yourself before. What you do and think now determines what you will be. So it doesn't matter if no one notices the good you do. Do it for God. Answer only to God.

Our lessons are structured in the laws of reality. The pain is that we live out our own misconceptions.

The fire of the law exists with supreme indifference: You can misuse the law to burn yourself; you can use the law to keep warm.

Never view difficulties as punishment. See them as lessons. We are here to learn. The lesson is that we are all one, and that God is the fundamental One.

THINK OF LIFE AS MOVING on several levels. Our past actions determine how we are born into this matrix. Where we are born and the time we are born thus make us susceptible to some energies and resistant to others. We are placed in the matrix to learn pre-set lessons. Thus, at certain times of our lives, we experience a great deal of pressure.

The pattern and the energies of our lives are set. The way we deal with them is not. We have free will within certain patterns of life, and we ourselves chose those patterns. We can do whatever we choose. As part of God, we have free choice. We can fall or rise. No one else can choose for us. No one else will. Even in a small choice is awesome power.

As long as we live solely on the physical level, believing it to be the total reality, we will respond most intensely to those pressures upon us. When we realize God is the creator of the universe and the reality, when we understand that we are individual expressions of that force, when we lose the sense of the little ego self, we free ourselves from those pressures.

If we continue to be locked in at the physical level, if we think that our bodies are the sources of life, if we think we have to have three meals a day, eight hours' sleep a night, and think that people have to talk to us in a certain way, if we have a great concern over what happened yesterday and what will happen tomorrow and are terribly worried about how we are going to get through life — as long as we are on that level, those energies bind us.

We aren't prisoners unless we choose to be.

9. Life goes on; we go on with it

The lives we live on earth remind me of a big department store. In one life we are in pots and pans. In another we are in rugs. In another we are in jewelry.

In each place, we will come in contact with the same people. If we do our jobs well enough in each place, I suppose eventually we will be able to work in the head office and keep files.

Q: If we have lived before, why don't we remember that?

A: Some do. There are many accounts and studies of people who have remembered things from other times.

Q: But most of us don't remember those lives.

A: True, most don't. The memory would be confusing. We barely remember our infancy, but all the information is there. When one achieves mastery of body, mind and spirit, one merges with God and memory of all past individualized existence is revealed. This is the only proof that need satisfy you.

Q: *That idea is hard for Westerners to accept.*

A: Disbelieving something won't make it untrue any more than believing something will make it true. It is more useful to exemplify values than to argue theory. Love God, and the truth will reveal itself.

Q: *Many people would like to think they will come back.*

A: That is the pitfall of desires.

Q: *Why a pitfall?*

A: Because the Earth is not our home. God is home. We are all here to learn a lesson. We can learn it any time. Some learn it when they are still babies. Some when they are old. Some never learn it.

We can learn about that energy pattern we were locked into at birth by overcoming our fears and doubts.

Once we understand that lesson and modify our behavior, we break free of those energy patterns. This triumph is disorienting. After that we may not feel quite at home in this life, but we will be more helpful to others and to ourselves, because we are no longer imprisoned by our misconceptions.

10. What you give, you get

WHAT YOU DO comes back to you. It may take a long, long while, but your action will finally make the rounds. What you give, you get. It is the basis of the world at this level.

Whomever you are with is someone you have been with life after life. You are with those people for a purpose, to learn a lesson or receive the blessings from your past actions. That is why you can meet people and instantly feel positive or negative toward them, even before you speak with them. You can feel their energy and remember.

Once a young man came to me, and I could see his life was very difficult. I realized that his current life was the final one in which he would simply be working out the problems he had created in the lives of others when he was an Egyptian pharaoh. As a pharaoh, he had ordered a great deal of terrible work, with no consideration of other human beings. The torment he had caused was so great that ever since he had been experiencing the same kinds of conditions he had caused.

Q: What did that mean? That he had to suffer?

A: It meant he had to learn the suffering caused by the ruthless imposition of power. Once a person has recognized this, he would be more judicious in his behavior. We are all one. This person could not go forward in his development until he had endured some of the hardship he had inflicted. When we overcome those old misconceptions and reactions, we arrive at what some call "the seedless state," and we can act without creating more problems for ourselves.

Q: How do we know what stage we are in?

A: The fact that we are all here together means that we are in basically the same place. We may seem very diverse, but we are one. Consider the world and all the people in it. You may think you meet people by chance. It is not by chance at all. We are all working together. Once we become free of these limitations, we work at the finer levels, what some call heaven. Otherwise, we must learn at the physical level.

At the time of our death, we make very accurate assessments of our lives. They are like subconscious films. All the major moments of our life are vividly recalled. We realize what we learned, what we didn't learn, what we did, what we failed to do. With that evaluation we begin to shape the challenge and lessons of our next life.

Reality has many levels, what a scientist might call frequencies. The physical level is the grossest, the most limiting. When you purify your heart and mind, the vibration of your senses increases and you may tune into those frequencies.

The man who was a pharaoh realized, at a certain level of his consciousness, that he had to overcome the suffering he had created. That is why I want you to realize that you are co-creators of the future with God, that you have free will, and that you can choose to make your future a thousand times better by being aware of the divine potential in you right now. This awareness will change your future and give power to your present.

THE MORE YOU CONCENTRATE ON DOING WELL what is before you, so that no one has to come behind you and do it over, the more your work is an offering, then you are not creating karma.

We can develop to the point where we choose to serve God — the God within us and within all. When we do that, the God in us guides us. Thus guided and guarded, we can come back to help others go forward.

The primary ambition of life should be to do the best you can every day. That will make life better. What you were no longer matters. What you are is vital. Realize eternity, but concentrate on now.

Q: You mean we must return to the suffering?

A: It depends on what you want to look at. If you give energy to the suffering, then it is suffering. If you give energy to the love and beauty, it is loving and beautiful. Choose. Remember what is beautiful and loving. Don't hang onto the pain. Thornton Wilder, the playwright, said that devotion to an ideal can make an entire lifetime pass like a pleasant dream.

11. Life is a school

LIFE IS a learning process. We are free when we realize our divine nature. This is not an achievement of the intellect. It must be a direct experience.

Years ago, I used to get so distressed with the suffering and anxiety in the world, particularly during World War II. At that time we lived in Springfield, Ohio.

One day there appeared the spirit of a young man who had been killed in France. He sat in our basement for a long time. (This dislocation sometimes occurs when a person is killed very suddenly.) My husband thought — well, he didn't really believe me. Anyway, this entity finally realized he was no longer on the physical plane. This is not uncommon to those who are "dead" since those we call dead still have life and look the same to themselves. This soldier then progressed on.

It occurred to me finally that if God wanted to, He could change it all in an instant. So if He didn't change it, there had to be a good reason. The reason, I came to recognize, was that the whole process of life is schooling.

YEARS AGO, I thought I was going to change the world and make things better. So when people came to me with problems, I deliberately intervened in their lives by softening whatever was bothering them.

Later, as I was about to intervene for someone, I felt as if I had been hit on the back of the head. That awakened me.

I realized that what seemed to be suffering and misery were ways for people to become stronger.

I realized that to deprive them of their experience would be to deprive them of a chance to gain strength and courage and insight that not only would make their lives better, but also would allow them to share those strengths with others. Without the suffering, they would not have those strengths, for this was the only way they could learn.

Now, I am not saying that we should neglect those in hardship and pain. I am talking of personal problems one might have caused by wrong thinking, problems that must be overcome through inner strength and awareness. After all, we help our children as much as possible and try to teach them how to avoid pain, even if there are some instructions they might not accept or understand. We love them but know that they will have to learn some things from experience; they are not willing to learn in any other way. The same is true of adults.

I DON'T LIKE SUFFERING. So while I realized that suffering might be a learning process, I begged to be shown ways that, if I couldn't deprive people of their lessons, I could help make their lives fuller and richer, so that they could progress more quickly.

So I cannot intervene. But I try to help others see so they don't have to learn the hard way.

IF YOU HAVE DIFFICULTIES, they are ways of working out your growth. If you deal with challenges as lovingly as possible, they will work themselves out. No matter how grim things look, they are on the way to a solution.

WHEN I TALKED TO SOME HANDICAPPED CHILDREN, I thought of how, years ago, it would have been an overwhelming experience. Now I understand that, no matter how severe these difficulties appear, they are in but a moment of time.

A handicapped boy I talked to, about 14 years old, was dying. He had to rest often; he resisted everyone. I recognized that in his past three lives, he had died suddenly, consequences of killings by him in his earlier incarnations. He had not been able to make a thorough transition from the physical to the reality and back, which we all must do. The child had not been able to retain the value of lessons he had learned. A slow death gave him time to develop more inner awareness.

Thus this was an opportunity to go slowly. What appeared to be a tragedy was a grace he had earned.

WE MUST LIFT OUR ATTENTION to a finer level and recognize the full extent of our existence. Though we must help relieve suffering, and must never hurt others, we must also refuse to be discouraged. Help one another, but go beyond the suffering.

There is another level of awareness. There is greater reality than you see. Once you reach this, you achieve a continuous feeling of joy and awakening. This is what Jesus meant when he said he could "look on tempests unafraid." They aren't tempests anymore. They aren't difficulties. They are ways of becoming. They are you.

SOMETIMES YOUR ORDEAL is very trying. Sometimes your circumstances are like a test to see if you will persevere. Many times I have said to God, "I absolutely will not give up."

When you mean business, when there is no way you are going to get too discouraged or unhappy, you may find that the ordeal stops. There is no point in it when you're not going to give up. The lesson has been learned.

If you can't control what happens outside of you, control what happens inside. After Job went through all his trials, you know, he was told "that thine own right hand can save thee."

Know what your own right hand can do.

Truth

We can only
Believe in love
If we are
Loving.

We can only
Believe in kindness
If we are kind.

We can only
believe in truth
if we are truthful.

The tragedy
Of lying
Is that
We can never
Believe
Anyone
Else.

You are more than the body

1. See people as energy

HUMANS ARE MADE UP of matter and energy. We are more than the body, more than the conscious mind.

Once you perceive that, you realize the resources at your command. You realize that the body is but an instrument of spirit. The body is merely condensed energy. After all, a piece of flesh appears that way only to your eyes. Under a powerful microscope the flesh is seen as a swirl of atomic particles.

As I have told you, you meet people in life after life. They will look different. They may be men in one life, women in another, but the energy of their personality, and the way it affects you, will basically be the same.

Thus it is helpful if you see people as fields of energy with which you must deal. If you can do this well enough, you will find that you don't have to become unhappy or angry with them. You won't need to wonder why Mary and Bill act the way they do. You just deal with the energy.

Science explains that much energy for physical life on this earth comes from the sun. The food you eat is energy captured by plants and animals, in addition to the finer energy you draw into yourself. If you can realize that you are part of the universe, part of the whole — that you are not little free-floating things, but that you are an integral part of the universe, vital — you will realize there is no insignificant life. All life is part of the cosmic ecology. Every thought you think is important. Because thought is energy, it is just as real as matter, since matter is only energy condensed and energy is the thought of God condensed.

Your mental, spiritual and physical habits form an energy pattern. If those habits and energies are nourished and directed by your spiritual awareness, the three energies focus like a laser and give great power. Thus it is helpful to exercise daily the body by exercise, the mind by thinking creatively and the spirit by prayer and meditation.

It is also important that you live according to the values you believe in so your physical, mental and spiritual lives mesh. If these three levels are not in harmony, they turn on one another, and the imbalance causes a disruption that comes out as anxiety, unhappiness, illness or a similar disturbance.

Too often we do not listen to the inner voice. We abuse the body by laziness and self-indulgence. We stunt the mind. We fail to acknowledge the spirit.

We must find ways of fulfilling ourselves without having to go shopping and riding around in cars and chewing each other in a gossipy kind of way. Don't get so caught up in the little things of life. We are like butterflies, you know, flitting from one inanity to another. Don't take petty things so seriously. Do well. Listen to your soul. And know. Think of eternity. Infinity. Be big. Be big.

The mind
has its limits
Unknown to the heart.
Lakota Sioux say,
"White man cannot be trusted,
Only speaks from the mind."
Truth comes from the heart.
The mind cannot comprehend
Infinity,
Where the heart is home.

2. Change the vibration

SINCE PEOPLE are made up of matter and energy, and since the mental, physical and spiritual habits create a vibration, this energy pattern becomes like the radio beam along which airplanes travel. The intuitive recognition of this beam, this direction, is divination.

This does not mean we are acting out a script some other force has written; it means we have established a pattern that, to some extent, makes us predictable for those who can sense the direction of these energies. There are thousands of years of legitimate history for various means of divination, but in the Age of Reason — and because of charlatans — these practices and abilities were discredited.

It is useful to recognize that our energies flow in a certain way mainly so we can know how to change that energy pattern if necessary. There are several ways to do that: through discipline, meditation, devotion, diet and so on.

Some methods are extremely powerful. For example, if you always heed and speak the truth, absolutely and precisely, without deviation, then you so align your soul and words that the words attain power. If you, in that state of attunement, tell someone, "You will go to Africa tomorrow," they will go to Africa tomorrow.

Many superstitions are merely psychological. Those can be crippling when a person allows them to govern the life. Other beliefs are valid because they originate in an awareness of subtle energy patterns. Learn to distinguish between the two, and to recognize that the greatest power possible is attunement with God.

REMEMBER, AS YOU DEVELOP, not to fall into the delusion that you are the source of power. Power is available to you, but all power comes from God. The greatest power is love. Of all the miracles Christ performed, the most profound was his ability to love and forgive while being crucified.

With God's love coming through you, you build strength and security in life. This is not accomplished overnight; this is not simply a matter of learning incantations. Prayers, yes, will give some power. But growth is little by little. It is like climbing a mountain. You know the cliff is in front of you and you chisel a little place, and you step. You carve another niche and move up. After a while you turn around and cannot believe how far you have come.

All you have to do is be aware of God.

All of you can do it. And I know that all of you will be very helpful to many people.

3. Knowledge we acquire; truth we realize

THERE IS A DIFFERENCE between knowing, believing and realizing. We can believe anything. Knowing has limitations. Two and two will make four and it won't make anything else. But if you realize two and two makes four you can live on a budget. That is the difference between believing in the divine energy and realizing. When you realize that everything is all one, that realization overcomes fear and desire. There is nothing to fear if everything is part of you. There is nothing to desire if everything is part of you.

You can read all about religions and still not realize their essence. You must develop your own awareness so you can experience these truths and what the scriptures tell you of your own nature.

Knowledge we acquire. Knowledge helps us go to the planets. But realization of the truth is what makes us free and teaches us how to walk upon the Earth as a loving family of human beings.

4. Death isn't all that much

WHEN I WAS OLD ENOUGH to walk, but not yet old enough to talk, I realized where I was. I walked across the room and looked out the window. I saw the sky was empty and realized it was the Earth. I looked down — I was sure it was the Earth. I cried and cried and cried. Until I was six years old, I wanted to die, it was so unbearable here.

But when I was six I realized there was no way out.

It is better to put your mind to living.

DEATH IS NO MORE than an act change in a play. The story is continual. There is no way to stop it. It is in God.

A Chinese proverb speaks of three difficult challenges.

One is to keep a secret.

Another is to bear injustice silently.

The third is to know someday we will die.

Death is nothing. As a matter of fact, death is one of the best things that can happen to us, but I don't like to tell people this. I don't want them to rush off. Everybody stay to the end.

ONCE I WAS DYING in a hospital in Cleveland. In my room there were two beds, a big window and a mirror at the foot of my bed. I knew I was dying; it didn't seem like all that much, you know.

Then I saw this figure at the foot of my bed. It was like a person holding some kind of chalice. I knew there was something about drinking from the chalice that would wrap things up for me.

Then I realized the apparition was also me and that it despised the "me" who was lying in the bed. I had not done anything useful with my life. I was very self-indulgent when I was young. I could feel this absolute contempt.

I sat up in bed and thought, "I cannot die. I am going to have four sons." I was very ill, so the night nurse came in, and the apparition disappeared.

That was when I realized that the Self is the God in us, and it is to that Self that we are responsible. It is that Self that will inexorably judge us at the time of our death, and to which we cannot offer one shred of excuse.

Death has
Come again.
We will have
A memorial,
Always new,
Always entertaining,
Always a little false.
We all know
Death is here
To stay,
And not go with us
Back to God.

Change yourself

1. Be critical within

IF YOU are going to be critical, be critical of yourself.

If you are going to complain, complain to yourself.

If you are going to make the world better, make it better within yourself first. The accomplishment will reflect outward.

INTROSPECTION and self-reform are the most vital actions you can take, for your living is action. Here, within, you change the world. Not out there. The Bible says it is better to light a candle than to curse the darkness. You cannot beat back the darkness. Nor can you put your arms around a light and hold the light back. The light will radiate naturally.

You can turn on the light.

Turn on the light.

When we want people to behave the way we dictate, when we say to people, "You do so and so because I want you to," we are destructive. I know from my own experience. We are often harmful not by intending to be but by not thinking. We often hurt those we hold dearest, the last ones we would want to hurt.

Everyone believes he or she is perfect and has to put up with many people who are not. But if we really *knew* any person we would never envy them.

Love one another and behave. Behave. You all know how to behave. Don't expect others to behave. You behave.

ONE WAY TO END A FRIENDSHIP forever is to point out a person's hidden agenda. While this agenda may be apparent to everyone else, it is a mystery to the individual. Objective self-criticism could recognize this agenda, but this is a rare procedure for any person. Honest self-analysis is a painful process. Sometimes a traumatic event can cause people to see their own behavior. This, of course, can lead to freedom from this pattern in the future. This is why, in ashrams, convents and monasteries, so much emphasis is placed on watching one's own behavior and motives. The pressure of self-scrutiny is one reason people abandon the spiritual life. Yet it is true, as Lord Jesus says, "The truth will make you free."

I HAD A COUSIN who spent some time in Maine with a retired sea captain and his wife. Every time the couple's sons would go out the door, the sea captain's wife would say, "Mind your failings." And I said it to my children. At the gate of our failings we have to stand guard.

We all have 20-20 vision for what is wrong with other people's lives. George Bernard Shaw said that the tragedy of living was that any chambermaid would know him better than he knew himself. We can see why other people are unhappy. We can see why they are suffering. We can see that other people should not turn to alcohol or whatever. That is not going to do any good. The only thing that is helpful is to meditate and see within yourself what you yourself can do to improve and make life better.

WE ARE NOT GOING TO TRANSFORM the world like Joan of Arc on a big white horse. If you do just one little thing, that will lead to other improvements. It is more productive to be able to stop one bad habit than to be able to stop the sun.

The difficulty in life is ignorance — but not just the ignorance of others. Our ignorance is the problem. All we can do about others is love and help them.

It is very humiliating for one to accept the responsibility for one's own life. It is a thousand times easier to blame things on our friends, our surroundings or our relatives. But that does not carry us forward.

SOME FAULTS THAT DISTURB YOU when you see them in others are faults that have some resonance in you. When we dislike someone, sometimes we project onto that person what we do not want to recognize in our own behavior. Recognize the unconscious in yourself and you will become more responsible in your behavior. Make sure that whatever you find difficult to deal with in others, you do not do yourself. For example, if you are repelled by the dishonesty of others, and you want to help overcome dishonesty in this world, be scrupulously honest yourself.

Don't be critical of others. Take the attitude that everyone has a right to be where they are. From there, they will all get to God. We will all get there.

THE DEVELOPMENT of your own inner awareness is like turning on a light. How far it shines is beyond our comprehension.

During World War II, some planes could bomb accurately if they had just four candle lights to pinpoint. We do not know how much we can do or how far our light shines.

2. Others must ask

WHEN WE WANT TO CHANGE SOMEONE but are not invited to do so, it is very difficult to realize that to do nothing is to do something. It is particularly difficult for Westerners. We have built into ourselves the habit of calling for horses to ride off into the sunset.

IF YOU HAVE A CHILD with a broken toy, you should let him fool around with it as long as the child wants to. You do not really know if the child is really interested in repairing it. As long as he is fooling around with the toy, the child is learning. He is learning at his own rate.

But if the child brings you the toy and says, "Please help me fix it; I don't know how," then you can help him. Yet one would be reluctant to go to the child and say, "Sit down and let me show you how to fix this toy." If you did that, the child might rebel and dislike the toy and perhaps dislike you for imposing yourself.

One of the most important restraints in life is to allow life to be, when no one is being harmed. Allow the other person his or her life.

DO NOT THINK that a person is like this or that. Though you see that person's outward behavior, you do not know the person's soul. Because God is in that person, the person is a mystery we do not know. Yet if we listen, we will hear. If we look, we will see.

When we practice the presence of God, the scales fall from our eyes, and we see it is God's world, and we do not know how it works. We do not know what people will say. We do not know what people will do. When we practice the presence, we do not require people to live in a particular way.

IT IS BETTER to love someone and let them live than try to influence their behavior by ordering them around. Sometimes it is very hard to be silent and let everyone live. When a person is annoyingly vulgar or mean, or if we have supervisory responsibility for that person, then we definitely should speak up and say, "You can do that if you like, but not here."

But we cannot tell people how they should live unless they ask. This is a very difficult discipline. When you know so well what would make a person's life simpler and happier, it is hard to just let people go.

But refraining from imposing our beliefs and advice on people is a submission to God's will. When the person asks for advice, we can give it. Until then, we must respect the person. This is an aspect of humility. It is very hard to be silent when you know, and know you know. It is in these small deaths of our ego that we come alive.

3. Choose not to suffer

A QUICK WAY TO ADVANCE in spiritual awareness is through suffering, because suffering is immediate.

The process of freeing ourselves is very much like housebreaking a dog. The dog associates pain and paper. While we are partially divine, we also learn very much as did Pavlov's dogs.

If you are on the spiritual path, this part of your development becomes easier to deal with and not so painful. To fall into suffering unknowingly can become very discouraging.

To suffer, you have to make a connection. If a person says to you, "What in the world are you doing that for?" you have to say, "Why in the world is he criticizing me?" in order to make a connection. If, no matter what people say, you think, "That is their opinion and they are entitled to it" — and think it without making a connection — you cut yourself loose from the pain.

Realization cuts connections. Realization is freedom.

We can overcome anything in life. We do not have to accept the suffering. Though it is true that suffering can help us grow, if we become anchored to suffering, we get lost in the woods, you see. When we recognize suffering and say, "This is suffering, but I choose not to do it," relief comes instantly like feeling the wave of cool air on which people walk when they go over the hot coals.

Be grateful in the morning that you have been able to sleep. Be grateful that you are alive. In this life, if you can walk and talk and see and hear, and are not suffering physical pain, you have a lot to be thankful for.

Difficult as the Earth is, suffering is very much like grabbing nettles. If you grasp them, they are not painful. If you just keep poking at them, they hurt.

George Bernard Shaw said that anything that does not kill us makes us stronger. If you have challenges, learn, be thankful and think, "It is not difficulty — it is all schooling." Learn. Be grateful to God for the opportunity to learn.

You can learn not to be tired, not to be hungry, not to feel deprived.

Realize that you are loved beyond comprehension. Realize that you are not suffering in some vacuum. Realize that God knows every decision that you make; that you are never alone.

You do not have to suffer. You have to learn. Suffering is simply a hard way to learn. If you concentrate on the learning, you don't have to go through all the suffering. I don't have a great thing for suffering. I don't like it.

IF YOU LEARN that you live in a universe, locked and contained, you realize that the universe is not merciless. The universe is simply impartial.

What seems to us to be incredible suffering and misery beyond our ability to endure is only ignorance.

Don't look inward and say, "Oooh, it's too much!" and then fall into despair. Little by little, everything in the world is accomplished. Little by little, we are freed. Little by little, suffering is overcome. If we begin with one small effort, then proceed to another and another, we come at last to the crest of virtue.

The universe runs on laws. The laws work as surely as gravity. Whether you know the spiritual laws or not, the laws operate precisely the same. As you come to realize the certainty of the laws, you can use them.

SUFFERING HAS a basic cause — the illusion of our separateness from God. We are all part of the One. The more you practice seeing everyone as part of the One, you will go beyond questions, beyond limitations. You will recognize what is true. You will not fall so easily into the trap of the glamours of the physical life.

You should not allow yourself to be so limited by the body. Think of yourself as a drop of water in the ocean. As long as the little drop thinks of its limitation, it is limited — a little drop of water. When the drop gives up the idea of its limitation and realizes it is part of the ocean, it becomes aware of the waves falling on the shore, of the whales in the deep, of the sun and the dark. It is still the drop of water, but its awareness has merged with the ocean. That is what meditation will lead to.

MANY TIMES IT IS EASIER to endure your own pain than the pain of those you love. You can just put your own pain in the freezer and think of it tomorrow. Feeling the suffering of others is not so easy. Love them. Help. If you cannot relieve suffering across the world, do your part by refusing to add to it. That is more helpful than agonizing over it.

The only purpose of suffering is to give you a sense of reality. When you gain that sense of reality, everything falls into place, because you see it from the awareness of God. This awareness is a conception entirely different from the one we usually have in our day-to-day life.

At first, though, this awareness — of what is real and what is not, of what is important and what is not — is wrenching, disturbing. Yet this awareness gives you freedom, absolute freedom, because you know reality is one, all the same — living or dead, here or there, prison or paradise; all the same.

ONCE YOU REALIZE the creative and collective power of the mind, its tangible effect on things physical, you realize that even what seem to be chance natural catastrophes are connected with our collective thoughts. Jesus demonstrated the power of mind over the elements when he calmed the sea. Only thought separates us from paradise. People think an arbitrary God unleashes floods and earthquakes, or that nature is separate from us. Thus people simply endure tragedies without realizing that we are all part of the One, and these things continue.

IF YOU SACRIFICE, accept it as a discipline.

If you endure hardship, accept it as an opportunity for strength.

If you suffer or are lonely, learn from it. Don't go around moaning, "I hurt! I hurt!" We all hurt. Sometimes very badly. But moaning all the time isn't going to carry life forward. It is better to say, "Yes, indeed, I hurt," and get on with the next task. Don't make a big thing of it so that you are bowing your head to suffering. Bow only to God; take the rest of it in stride.

Know that, no matter what you are going through, thousands have gone through the same thing. Millions would love to be in your place.

We are so blessed with food and comfort that we don't realize how much anguish and suffering are in the world.

We make our demons.

We make our hells.

We make our sorrows, because they are a way for us to learn.

We cannot always avoid the difficulties that are part of an enormous pattern, but we can be sustained through them.

Anything that helps you overcome sadness, anything that makes life bearable, is a valid, valuable experience.

You have to put your mind to dealing with difficulties in a loving way. If you do it well, you won't have to do it again.

4. Love one another

YOU HAVE TO LEARN TO LOVE as you learn to play a violin. Though we may be born with a talent for music, we are not born knowing how to express it perfectly. The emotion of love is natural, but refinement is often necessary, because love has become so confused with pleasure.

Whomever you love, recognize that it is the God in them that you love. Love should be a triangle between you, God and the person. If it is only between you and the person, your fulfillment is limited. If you get hung up on the idea that the person is what you love, the expectation becomes an insatiable hunger that cannot be satisfied, because it is not real.

If you become enamored with the way another person sees you, that is infatuation. You are in love with an image of yourself. It is like looking in a mirror; you are not conscious of the other person. You are simply conscious of the benign image, and you want it to stay that way. It will not. Eventually, that image will change. There is much agony in that. See God in everyone, and love God in everyone. That is the way to expand love.

WHEN WE LOVE SOMEONE we become aware of the needs of others more than our own needs. In gratitude we also gain a more balanced awareness of our lives. As we develop awareness we become centered. That is, we know who we are and what we are doing and why. We are also totally responsible for all of our actions. Becoming centered overcomes fear and desire.

Q: It is very hard when we really have to love each other. There are so many different ideas of the word love.

A: Love works like this:

If you love a person, you must not make a judgment.

If you make a judgment, you must be compassionate.

If you cannot love, and make the judgment, and are not compassionate, you will experience the same judgment yourself. Whether in this life or another, you will be brought back to the same circumstances you created yourself. You will wonder why you were judged that way.

Any time that you find that people do not see you as you are, and you are faced with what you think is an outrageous attitude on the part of others, recognize it as a judgment you yourself have made before. Realize how unjustified it is. Absorb into yourself all the calumny, humiliation or whatever, and say to God, "I understand."

The karmic lesson will end.

But if you become outraged and say, "Why should I have to endure this?" you are simply perpetuating the same condition.

Q: *That could go on endlessly.*

A: Yes. We have eternity. But there is a better way to use it.

WE CAN GO LIFE AFTER LIFE and never experience love. We learn to love by coming into contact with love. Recognize love as an expansion of consciousness, a divine gift.

At this point, we love those to whom we are married, our children, or others with whom we are close. As we expand our love, we learn to see and feel ourselves in everyone.

Help others. That doesn't mean you have to be a mindless do-gooder, but make your life purposeful. Make the best possible use of your time, and let others live. Eventually you will find you spend a great deal of time thinking of other people.

Q: Sometimes love is simple — until some obnoxious or spiteful person comes along; that kind of person is hard to love.

A: Speak as clearly as you can to the God in them, but don't get caught up in what people say or whether they understand you.

Q: Whether or not they understand?

A: I think we become overly sensitive.

Q: To what they think of us?

A: Yes. You know, I have some friends who are very, very difficult. Their difficulty lies in their own non-acceptance of love and life. They try to make life the way they think it should be rather than the way it is. Years ago this sort of energy was a problem for me. I felt diminished by constantly trying to deal with it. Now it never bothers me, because I realize it is their way of living. You can be as supportive as possible without accepting the way they beat on you with words, blow by blow.

Say what you want, clearly and with love. If they react harshly, that is their way of reacting; it is not your way of speaking. None of us is responsible for the way others react. We are responsible only for what we think and say. Being one, we are alone in life with God.

SOME PEOPLE ARE AFRAID OF LOVE because it makes them vulnerable. They would rather not love at all than be placed in that position. When we accept the vulnerability and just go on, we progress.

THE CONSCIOUSNESS WITHIN US is infinite, and love has an infinite reach.

Once I had a little dog that I took in to allow his leg to heal. He ruined some of our furniture. I took him to my aunt, but he tormented my aunt's small dog. Finally, my aunt gave him to another woman, who lived alone in a big house.

Three weeks after she got the dog, the house caught on fire in the middle of the night. The little dog barked, woke her up and saved her life by taking her to safety.

So do everything with love, knowing that no matter how insignificant your action seems to you or how difficult your effort is, in the vastness of time it will turn out to be good. It doesn't matter whether we are there to witness.

We are part of the universe. If we just function well in our little part, everything will be better.

5. Make up your mind to be happy

YEARS AGO, I discovered that people were as happy as they made up their minds to be. In my own life, I was very, very unhappy for a long time. As a child I wanted to die, for I did not want to be on this Earth. Finally, one day before I got up from my bed, I thought to myself, "From now on, I am going to have a happy life."

My life was transformed. The same things happened, but I put all my energy into the things that were pleasant and that I enjoyed; I didn't give energy to the times I didn't feel good. Even physical pain can be held to a certain level.

The little ego sits in front of the great, huge Self. The Self is the immortal part, the God in us. The ego says, "I'm hungry. I'm tired. Suzy hasn't said a kind word about me." Forget it. Realize, "God, God, God."

Money cannot make you happy. Wine cannot make you happy. What makes you happy, really, is the intention to be glad. Of course, good heath, productive work and loving friends matter. Even so, you must work from the inside out rather than wait for the outside to become exactly as you want it to be.

Q: Some people are very unhappy, yet are surrounded by pleasant things. Why can't they resolve their problem?

A: Some people have a very rigid concept of the world, and their concept has nothing to do with the way life really is.

We are all caught in the web of our habits, our own thinking. One way to overcome this is to direct our energies toward God so everything we do is an offering. At first, this way of thinking seemed like death to me. I was so miserable that everything seemed to me a helpless condition, even to expect to be happy. So I just thought about activity.

I found out, after some years, that I was very happy. I could look back and not have to say, "I wish I had not done that." We don't come to this kind of loving until we surrender the ego.

MOST OF US SPEND a great deal of time thinking so-and-so thinks this or that, then we deal with that in our minds. This kind of thinking consumes much energy and time, and it has nothing to do with taking life forward. We should resolve to be happy, to have some purpose in our lives, then do something every day to bring that about. We don't have to be a victim of love. We don't have to be unhappy. It's all part of a dream anyway.

6. Look beyond your little melodrama

DR. CARL JUNG SAYS that the Self — the inner energy we all have the same amount of — is like a general in charge of an army. The general knows what the battle is all about and how it can be won. But his orders go through a long chain of command to the conscious mind, the foot soldier, who is only aware of the rain and the mud and is tired of the whole thing and doesn't want to be there anyway. When we concentrate on what needs to be done, we are in touch with headquarters.

MOST OF US are always caught up with our little self, locked into all this inner activity, never seeing the sun rise or set. We don't hear or see God's marvelous world because our own little drama is so turbulent that we cannot quiet it down.

We should look into our lives and decide what our little drama is. Do we want people to see us as the best organized person in the world? Do we want to be seen as having the most exquisite taste? As being the most intelligent? As the one most able to make money? As the best cook? As the greatest lover?

Once we decide what we really want to express we begin to have some sense of reality in our lives.

We suffer because we cannot get the recognition from others that we feel our little drama deserves. It causes us enormous suffering when we realize that our drama — which can be anything — doesn't mean very much at all to others. They do not care if we are the greatest student, artist, cook, teacher or lover.

Many of us think of our families as an audience. We expect them to be devoted. We feel they should be concerned over our daily performance. We think they should bear witness to our progress in life. We hold them responsible for making us happy or unhappy. The truth is that we are alone in life with God.

Therefore if we see God in everyone and everything, our daily life will change. When we realize it is all God, we know we are not doing anything. God does everything.

IT IS WE WHO BLIND ourselves. Our enemy lies within. When we overcome the enemy within, we overcome the world.

We can do this through meditation.

We can do this through awareness.

We can do it by loving others more than ourselves.

WE MUST ALWAYS be aware in life of this desire for power. It is a drama that closes off the rest of the world to us. Often, when we love people, we want them to act in a certain way, not so much because we think that acting in that way is such a great thing, but because we simply like for people to do what *we* want them to do. This is a heady wine, very dangerous.

We have to learn to submerge ourselves, to be aware of others and see legitimately where they are and why they feel as they do.

Most of us are aware of why we feel as we do. We are aware of different things that occurred to us in childhood, experiences that influenced us.

When we can slow down our little interior melodramas and recognize that other people have these same melodramas — that they are suffering, that they are feeling things we are not aware of — then, in a true sense, we are dying to achieve life.

Dream's end

The terrible death
Is the death in life
When there is
No body to bury,
No hymns to be sung,
No flowers to grace a grave.

There is no
Gathering for grief,
No touching hands
Against the lonely dark.

How terrible to bury
Beauty and Grace,
Strength and Loveliness
In the silent reaches
Of the mind
With only the heart
To be
Sentinel
For grief,
Its own candle
Burning.

7. Don't judge others

Q: YOU HAVE SAID that if one makes a harsh, unforgiving judgment of another, the person who judged harshly must experience that same thing?

A: Yes. You will come to a point where you have done everything you can, as well as you can, and you will be judged mercilessly and found wanting. It is a very harrowing experience. All of us go through it. It's very much as though the world is turned over. Yet the experience can also be a leap forward in learning.

If you want to learn in a more painless way, you can. For example, if you are a man, think of yourself as a woman, or vice versa, and consider your behavior. If you are a man, what would you think if a woman behaved the same way? This technique helps you to become objective, which is difficult. Self-knowledge is a most difficult accomplishment. By thinking of yourself as of another gender, or as of another race, or as another individual you admire, you can get a better perspective. Anything that gives you a little distance will help.

So don't criticize other people. Life is as difficult for them as it is for you.

It is very easy to judge. It is Godlike to be compassionate.

One great way to gain freedom in your life is to abandon criticism of others. In my own life this was very difficult. I did it as a discipline and had no idea of the enormous benefits that would come.

First it gives you freedom. Then it gives you a far greater understanding and perspective, because you learn to see people as they see themselves. If we see people from our own point of view and our own ignorance, they can seem very dull, and we limit people unfairly by our own conceptions.

We suffer from the idea that people are what they possess. Thus we are always wanting, wanting things. Our clothes, basically, should be to keep us comfortable. If we judge others by their clothes, we are defeating ourselves. Look at the person and love. If you love, you won't say, "Why are these people wearing those awful things? I can't stand it." Just love others and allow them their lives. True love lets everybody live.

A loving acceptance of others frees you from criticism.

8. Don't have expectations

I FINALLY REALIZED that it is personal virtue that gets you out of all this — not virtue for the sake of virtue, but right activity, activity that harms no one. It is being observant of your own behavior and accepting that everyone else is doing all they can that makes life bearable. Having no expectations of others is freedom.

In a larger sense, I have no friends, I have no enemies. I live in God's world where there is true equality. I am totally responsible for the way I treat others. I am not responsible for the way they treat me.

IT SEEMS TO ME that some people who were neglected as small children — not given praise for their work or recognized as trying to be helpful — grow up to procrastinate more than those who felt more rewarded in their childhood. This procrastination can be a real burden, an obstacle to a rewarding life. When a person decides to take full responsibility for one's own life and happiness, health and well-being, this habit of procrastinating is gradually overcome. The conquest comes not by recognizing the cause of procrastination, but by taking a different attitude to life itself. Procrastinating seems to be a way of putting off the unpleasant moment of feeling one has worked for nothing. When one becomes one's own best friend, the joy of accomplishment becomes the main issue. There is more indifference to recognition or praise of one's work and more satisfaction in what has been accomplished. Seeing the work done well is reward enough. It is a question of whether one wants praise or accomplishment. It is human to want both.

EXPECTATIONS ARE AMONG the really damaging attitudes in life. We crucify ourselves on our expectations. People waste vast energy and time fantasizing about life, expecting things to be just so. It is as though they have formed computer programs in their minds; when the outer world appears different from what the computer program projects, they are torn inside.

You really are much better off living and loving God and doing your best every day with whatever is before you. The more you expect from life, the more you are setting yourself up for misery.

Expectation is different from planning. Planning is a purposeful way of using energy. Planning sets a goal. Goals can guide you. Fantasies can frustrate you.

Sometimes the most practical goal you can have is to get through the day. If you can get through the day, you can survive.

9. Exemplify what you believe

IT IS A GREAT PRIVILEGE to be alive in this place, difficult as it is, because here you can exemplify what you believe.

If you believe in love, you can be loving.

If you believe in truth, you can be truthful.

If you believe in kindness, you can be kind.

I always thought it was valuable for people to have a little theater experience because in theater one realizes that a role has discipline. If you're a student, be a student; don't wish you were a teacher. Then, when you are a teacher, be a teacher. Be what you are.

If you exemplify a virtue, such as truth or kindness, do not do it in the expectation that this virtue will come back to you from others. You will not necessarily be loved by others immediately because you are loving. That should not make any difference. Live with the awareness of God and speak with the realization that God is within you. Speak to the God in others and your life will be directed. It won't matter whether people like you or whether it is day or night.

We are born in this form to test our conceptions. It is easy to say, "I believe in unconditional love" until we come face to face with someone who, for whatever reason, dislikes us and makes a great effort to make our life miserable. When that happens, we must prove if we really believe in love. It is easy to love someone who sees us as the Queen of the May. We go forward when we love without reason. It is very humiliating, yet very instructive, to realize that life is beyond our conception — and yet love it anyway.

CONSIDER SERIOUSLY what you believe, and from that belief speak to others. From that belief, do what is before you. From this inner awareness, move, live, and have your being.

Mahatma Gandhi liberated India partly by having his men walk unarmed against the British soldiers. Many were killed, but finally the British were appalled at their own atrocious behavior, so they simply stopped. It was a victory for non-violence.

Non-violence doesn't mean that you are going to sit in the corner and be happy. Non-violent resistance requires that you stand up for what you believe and and that you be willing to die for your principles without harming others.

When people no longer remember the name of India — and most nations will have different names well into the future — people will remember, just as we do, Mahatma Gandhi, because he exemplified the great virtues in which he believed. He exemplified non-violence for the new world.

That is what I mean when I say you must live what you believe. By doing so, you give virtue a living power and become one with it. The wise know the truth; the realized become the truth.

10. Live courageously

YOU WILL FIND, as you get older, that all the things that terrified you and made you think, "Oh, if that happens, I will surely die," those things can happen time and again and you will not die. You will get stronger and far happier.

There is a great deal to be said for courage. Courage comes, very truly, from the "calloused scars of outlived despair." People become courageous because they realize that no matter how bad things are, they could always be worse. No matter what you go through — no matter how terrible, how humiliating, how difficult it seems — thousands have gone through such hardships before you. Those who have realized that God is God were able to survive courageously. The great triumph, as I have told you, is to survive.

It is no great thing to die. Anybody can die.

It is better to live.

That is the challenge. This took me years, years, years to learn.

IT TAKES A GREAT DEAL of courage to live. There are many fears — the fear of failure, of abandonment. We all deal with these fears in individual ways. We can overeat or steal or go shopping or take to our bed with sincere suffering.

Quite often a sense of spiritual security can overcome these fears. This spiritual awareness can be expressed in service to others. I don't think people go out of their way to suddenly serve others; I think the need appears and they respond. The usually unrecognized benefit is a loss of fear. That old saw, that "virtue is its own reward," is true.

A HELPFUL WAY to strengthen yourself is to face the things you fear the most.

If you fear death, face the idea of death, knowing your own immortality. Concentrate on the reality that death is but a transition.

If you fear illness or helplessness, concentrate on it and face it, and determine what you could still do.

Once you face these fears, they become insignificant, and you can continue living. True living is practicing the presence of God.

OUR ANXIETIES and fears come from our own refusal to live what we really believe in the depths of our soul. Fears are an inner misalignment.

The most invincible quality in the world is virtue — the virtue of being true to one's own Self. If you do something you don't really think is right, you become vulnerable.

Your threats and salvation are all inside you. They are not out there. Inside is the freedom. Inside is heaven. Work inside and the work out there will take care of itself. You have no control out there. You can't control what people say or think. Inside, you change the world. It is an inner conquest. We have done great work out there. Now we must do it in here.

YOUR SELF, THE SOUL, is immortal. As the *Bhagavad-Gita* says, fire cannot burn it, water cannot wet it.

Learn to meditate so you can find peace and contemplate the Self. The Self will answer anything, deliver you from anything. Knowing this is the wellspring of courage. The Self is your solace, your comfort, your guide. Nothing can dim it. Old, young, sick, well, the Self is always the immortal, shining light.

> Disaster
> Is some
> Large entity,
> Unexpectedly delivered.
> A place must be given,
> An acknowledgement
> Made.
> Total acceptance
> Will assimilate it to
> Nothingness.

11. Do it yourself

NO ONE IN THE WORLD can do these things for you. You can do them for yourselves. All the great masters have said the same thing: Love one another, see God in everyone; serve.

The more you open your heart, the more you love, the more you give, the more you have. Life works in a circular motion.

There is no way you can give away your last cent and not have it come back a thousandfold.

Don't be afraid — "If I say this, what will they think?" Forget it. With calm kindness be true to yourself and say whatever is in your heart. If you like someone, say so. If someone looks good, don't be afraid to tell them they look good. Don't wait to stand over some coffin and say, "I always liked her. She always looked so pretty — I wish I had told her."

We should all realize that there is no way we can live on the earth forever. So if there is anything that you want to get done, do it. Do it. Then when you go, you can go without regret.

MUCH UNHAPPINESS comes from just standing around the edge of the pool wondering what it would be like to jump in. We can go many lives just standing around the edge. When we just stand around the edge, we can be very unhappy and fearful. When we jump in, we swim.

ONE TRAGEDY of our thinking is the belief that it was all right for Jesus and Moses and Buddha and Krishna and all those saints to exemplify high standards because they lived up on Cloud 9 — but that here, where we are, things are different. So we think we can behave as we do because that is the way others around us behave.

In school a girl behind me was very good at Latin, so I couldn't see why she would not let me copy from her paper. She was a Girl Scout and said that I should be a Girl Scout because then I would realize that copying was wrong. I really had no morals. I didn't even know that I had no morals. Day by day I have come to recognize that there is an acknowledgment of the Divine and consequence in one's moment-by-moment behavior, and it's pretty heavy-duty. But it's only one's own duty. We don't have to worry about what others do — they are doing all they can. We don't know where others are.

12. Nowhere is someplace

ONE OF THE MOST marvelous things I was taught was that nowhere is someplace. It is all the same.

People waste so much energy and emotion thinking, "If I were only there, I would be happy," or, "If I were only with that person, I would be happy." Life is an illusion. It is all One. Being one, it is infinite. There is no loss, no gain. One day is like another — a string of pearls. All activity directed toward God becomes devotion, so it doesn't matter what it is — eating, sleeping, washing windows, talking — it's all the same. There isn't one thing that is more than another if you give them the same intense devotion. In that state of consciousness there is no place to go that is more than where you are. You can remove yourself from situations and influences that are detrimental, but God is everywhere.

Q: My father was somewhat religious, but also material-istic.

A: I don't think that matters. I think that what occupies a person's mind is often what is necessary for that person's development. We believe many things to be fundamental and essential to life, but as we become spiritually aware, these things matter less.

The painful part of spiritual growth is not the spiritual part but the separation that occurs. I know when I talk to people, it isn't what I tell them that is painful, but there is this wrenching over something they have assumed to be true. When that assumption is knocked out from under them, other assumptions must fall.

When I was a little girl, my cat got sick. I took it to a Christian Science church to get it healed. The church was not like my own Sunday school, which was warm and had cookies. The Christian Science room was bare, and the teacher seemed severe. Yet the healing that I witnessed taught me that the way things look sometimes has very little to do with reality. It taught me that, where one might least expect it, there would be help.

13. Love yourselves, too

BE TRUTHFUL AND HONEST about all you think and feel, say and do. Then you have a sense of freedom from your own self. You are not an enemy to you.

Be good to yourselves. I don't mean that you should be self-indulgent any more than you should be self-pitying, but acknowledge the God in you. When you do something that is difficult, whatever it is, you may be the only person who knows how difficult it is. Tell yourself, "That's good. Keep it up." Do something so that the inner self doesn't feel it is alone on the mountaintop.

MANY PEOPLE who are kind and loving and supportive to their friends can be very cruel to themselves. Be kind.

Love the God in you. If you are not your own best friend, who will be? The greatest thing in the world is goodwill.

14. Cherish your time

GUARD your time. This moment is a treasure. Don't give a minute to something that does not make you happy. Don't endure boredom. Don't endure anything that makes you feel less.

SOMETIME WE THINK that if we go to a party or to a movie we will be happy. Then we find out that it does not really make us happy. So always evaluate your day. What was the most productive part of it? What was the most helpful?

See what you really enjoy, and make more of it in your life. If reading makes you happy, make more time for reading. If it's painting, paint. We can — without more money, without more friends — make our lives happier by simply being more aware of what makes us happy and by making room for that in our lives.

DEVELOP AWARENESS so that you always are in the moment, not in the future, not in the past. Only in the moment. And know that every moment counts. Every moment offers the opportunity to find God, to recognize God, to see the various forms of God.

15. Be aware

IF YOU PAY ATTENTION to your life, if you learn to attune to your soul, vast information will unfold to you. If you develop your devotion, your concentration and your meditation enough, you can open your own intuition, which is the highest form of knowledge.

IT IS TERRIBLY IMPORTANT not to be taken in by one's fantasy. Fantasy can color the way we see others. We can create a whole scenario and act it out, with dire consequences. Watching our behavior can lead to self-awareness and self-honesty. If we were perfected we would not likely be here. This is a place to continually learn more.

IT IS IMPERATIVE to recognize one's emotions: what causes them; if they are helpful or destructive. Never be caught up in the behavior of others. There is nothing you can do about it. Know what *you* are doing and why.

Learn to watch life. Do what you feel is right and have no judgment of others. Their karma is their problem, not yours. Don't get into it. Remember, the mills of the gods grind slowly, but they grind exceedingly fine. We do not have to retaliate. Even thinking of the unkindness is foolish. Unkind people never think they are being unkind. Other people think their actions are either good or justified. To recognize our own evil and to outgrow it is what is helpful.

PEOPLE MAKE UP personal myths that will justify their behavior. A man I know lives in the fantasy that, had he not married, he would have become a doctor. This man takes a year to read one novel, but he is convinced his career was sacrificed for his wife. It would do no good to try to help this person see his myth as pure fantasy. It serves him a deep purpose.

If we face the truth about our lives, we will have much more control over our emotions, our health and even our finances. Our behavior will be normal. Just as importantly, we will learn from our experiences. The person who is caught up in fantasies and denial will not learn, but will instead project his feeling of failure onto someone else. Sometimes the person will blame life or God or relatives, and the experience is wasted.

Night and day　　　　　*A whole year*
Night and day　　　　　*Gone.*

16. Once aware, you cannot be lonely

I AM NOT USING a paradox when I say that we are all alone in life with God and we can never be lonely.

We are permeated with God. There is no way that we can be lonely once we thoroughly perceive this truth. There is no way that we can be fearful again.

We think we must have so many things — help or money or new clothes or affection. A saint once said we were like little fish in the middle of the ocean saying, "I'm thirsty, I'm thirsty." There is no way you can be thirsty. God is the source of all.

As the Psalm says, even if we make our bed in Hell, God is there. If we anchor ourselves to the realization of God, it does not matter where we are.

A WOMAN ASKED ME, "Is it true that if you burn a yellow candle such-and-such a number of days, you will find love?" My beloved darlings, you don't have to burn candles to find love. Your energy — the very life in your body — comes from God in the form of pure love.

Q: I DON'T MEAN to sound melodramatic, but I don't recall when I was not lonely. Was it meant for me to be lonely? Is that what I am supposed to learn?

A: No. The loneliness is a maladjustment in your mechanism that is not allowing your energy to be expressed as love. If you use your energy as love, it reflects back into your life. If not used as love, the misuse of the energy causes a defect, like a machine that doesn't work properly. Thus the energy distorts into fear and anxiety and loneliness all the time, regardless of where you are or the person you are with. This energy we project; we think it is "out there."

Q: *(Another person) Maybe he is just content with himself.*

A: That is not true loneliness — that isn't what he is speaking of. To be content alone isn't loneliness. We must not confuse loneliness with being with people or not being with people. One can be lonely in a crowd. Loneliness is a misuse of life energy.

17. No one owns another

BEING ALONE IN LIFE with God, none of us owns another. We should be responsible and loving but not possessive. However, we can appreciate the love others give us, knowing that, in its pure state, it is God's love.

You should not be jealous. Give your love without expectation, without undue attachment. That can be difficult if you believe that only two people can love each other through life. You will love this person, this person, this person. You should love them all because God is in everyone. Learn to love impersonally.

If you divinely love a person, no one, no one can interfere with your love for that person. You are responsible only for the love you give, not for the love someone else gives you. Pay attention to your love, which is untouchable, perfect. If someone else wants to feel love for the same person you do, they will have to love the person on their own time. Another place in the heart. Not your place. Not your time. You're free. Homeless, but free. Like birds, safe from falling.

Love goes beyond walls and space and the limits of time. The fact that we are all in the world is gratifying, but that we can love beyond the bounds of the world should be even more gratifying.

18. Silently absorb the qualities of others

ANY TIME we are with people — at the market or working or sitting or whatever — we imbibe from one another. That's why when you were little your mother said, "I don't want you to play with Johnny. He's not a nice little boy." We pick up from one another.

I have told you we are all energy and that there is an energy field around you, perceptible to some. This energy spreads to others and conveys love, tension or any other emotion. You partake of the energy of others by being around them.

Therefore choose to be around people who are happy, people whose lives uplift you. This is crucial for those who hope to persist on the spiritual path or who seek their own upliftment. Emotions are like measles: they catch.

One can advance and gain strength merely by being in the presence of a highly spiritual person.

WHEN YOU HAVE TO BE with an unpleasant person, you should still strive to be happy within. Where you have a choice, be with uplifting people. Absorb the strength and happiness that comes from them. Radiate joy yourself.

Similarly, if you wish to attune yourself to the qualities of saints and spiritual masters, study and contemplate their works. This is similar to tuning a radio to a particular frequency: The energy of a saint radiates and can be tapped.

19. You are like your friends

YOUR ENERGY ATTRACTS people to you in the same way a magnet attracts metal filings. So if you want to know what you are like, look at your friends. The friends you are with usually are going where you are going and doing what you are doing. Generally, you are working on the same level. Choose carefully those with whom you associate.

20. Bless others

IF YOU SEE SOMEONE who is ill or unhappy, remember that God is in you and in that person also. With that understanding, you can bless the person with whatever prayer you feel in your heart.

You can do this for anyone, whether you know the person or not. It is much more helpful to pray for the person than to see misery and agonize about it all the time.

Send good thoughts to people as you visualize or see them. Work silently with your mind and heart.

21. Be more

YEARS AGO, when I first studied painting, I had a marvelous instructor, and he told me, "You cannot paint more than you are."

We all paint with our lives. Be more to paint more.

22. Angry people speak to themselves

Q: WHAT IF ALL YOUR LIFE you have been taught that you aren't much, that you didn't "have it upstairs"? What if that has been imbedded in you?

A: Give that up. Anchor yourself to God, not to people.

Remember that whenever a person speaks unkindly to you, he speaks to himself. We are all here as witnesses, and we are all one.

If a person is angry or speaks unkindly, that person is suffering within. This is how we learn to be compassionate to people who are unkind. We know they are not really talking to us, no matter what they say, no matter how much it seems they are trying to hurt us.

Each of us is responsible for every idle thought, for every word we speak.

If you are angry, it is better not to say anything, for then you are not adding to difficulty.

If other people are angry, they are on their own time. They must stand in their own judgment.

So try to concentrate on your life so you realize how much your own actions affect others around you. Realize in your life how much you can love, how much you can serve, how much you can give, for only in these actions have you any control or responsibility.

VERY OFTEN you deal with people who literally do not know what they are doing. They are so locked into this personal dream of themselves and what they think they are doing that they really are not conscious of their behavior. You cannot confront them because the person you are aware of does not exist for them. Sometimes some extremely painful experience can cause them to become aware.

23. "Good" is a matter of direction

GOOD IS THAT WHICH LEADS US to the realization of our oneness with God. Evil is that which deceives us of our true nature.

Thus good and evil are, in a sense, matters of direction, not arbitrary edicts by God.

Evil can be recognized as the act of doing something that we would not want someone to do to us, except we feel justified in doing it because of someone else's behavior.

ONE SHOULD NOT be good simply to have people think he or she is good -- for the social glamour of being nice.

Follow your conscience and you will not have to wake up in the morning and say, "I hope I don't fall into temptation today."

Just cling to God. We do not overcome temptation by wrestling with evil so much as by holding onto something more. You could say that temptation is not overcome; it falls from us.

ANCHORED TO GOD, you cannot harm others. Others cannot harm you. Thus anchored, you can only make the world better. Otherwise there would be no point in serving God.

I would not take up your time except I know these things are true. If you will do them, your life will be simple, happy and richer than you have believed possible.

Q: WHAT IF YOU TRY and temptation still comes to you?

A: Anchor yourself to God, and whatever happens, happens. If you are anchored, I promise you that the result can only be good.

24. Serve

I ALWAYS FIXED my husband's breakfast. Later, I gave up coffee. After that, I found that when I fixed his breakfast, the coffee wasn't there. This was quite a jolt to me, because I had thought I was fixing his breakfast. I wasn't. I was fixing my own.

When we think of the needs of others beyond the point where they complement our own needs, we are serving God.

When you serve others, think of the God in you as the servant. Be a channel. Don't fool yourself into thinking that you are the source. Connected to the God within you, limitless energy can flow through you.

THE MOST PRODUCTIVE course is to concern ourselves with how we can help, here and now. I'm fond of the story about the man who died and, when he met Saint Peter, asked to see Hell. So Saint Peter took him to a place with a beautiful banquet table, yet the people were starving. The man asked Saint Peter why the people were starving with all that food around. Saint Peter answered, "They don't have elbows. They can't feed themselves." Then Saint Peter said, "Now I will show you heaven."

Saint Peter showed the man another beautiful dining room with fruits, flowers and music, but the people were happy and plump. The man said, "But they don't have elbows either."

"No," Saint Peter replied, "they feed one another."

Feed one another.

25. Don't be a doormat

JUST BECAUSE you love, it is not written anywhere that you have to be a doormat for other people to walk on. You do not return hate for hate, but you need not accept hate, either. In all the suggestions I give you, you must also be discriminating. Decide wisely what you can do and what you cannot.

Why be a mindless do-gooder? Just to be endlessly at people's beck and call is not intelligent. You should only accept responsibility for what you can bear. In considering and serving others, keep your balance.

Take responsibility for saying with an even mind that you will only tolerate so much. Do not allow the God in you to be humiliated any more than you would humiliate God in another.

26. Don't accept anything resentfully

MOST OF THE TIME you will find that you don't have to be with people who are disturbing to you. Your obligation is not to hate or hurt them, but you do not have an obligation to be around them unless some duty compels it. It is better to tell a person not to visit than to resent that person's coming.

A dear friend asked me if she could keep me company. I wanted to get some painting done, so I said "No." I knew that, unless she was a very extraordinary person, our friendship probably would end because of my response, but it is better to say "no" and not be tense and unhappy.

Remember that when you say A, then B follows. Some kind people find it hard to keep that in mind, but you are responsible for your own happiness.

So when you say "Yes," you should say and mean it cheerfully. When you tell a person, "I love you," you should mean it unconditionally. You shouldn't love them on the condition that they do this or that for you, or only if they are kind. You will love them no matter where or what they are. This is the kind of love and friendship you must give to one another. By so doing, you give those qualities of spirit to yourselves. It doesn't do any good, after all, to love people unconditionally if you are going to love yourself only partially.

27. Love must evolve

GOD ISN'T a Baptist or a Catholic or a Jew or Hindu or a Moslem. God is just God.

There is no intellectual way to know God. Don't be dogmatic. Don't worry about ceremonies and historical details and theological doctrines. To start, just love God.

Any way that you can conceive of God and realize that you are part of God is the way that will start you on the path home. On the way, don't become so attached to the path that you love the path more than God.

THERE IS NO WAY you can come to love God without loving a person or child or plant or animal or something else, because they are all in God.

We can sit around and talk about God from now to the end, you know. It is very fascinating, but just talking isn't really going to do any good. You must love God yourselves.

What changes us is not simply knowledge, but the capacity to realize truth and express it in our behavior.

We know the truth. Everybody knows. We have heard it from the time we began to hear, but most of the time we think that the truth applies to something or someone out there, somewhere else. We accept a separation between what we believe to be true and the way we must live.

Look into your hearts: What do you believe? What do you truly think makes life worthwhile? Then do it. Do it. Little by little. Give up doing what other people do.

And give up guilt. Guilt is like rust; it is not vital for living. People laden with guilt are suffering more from their reactions to life than to life itself. Thus they are caught up in something that is not real. They do this by putting out facsimiles of themselves. Would the crowd like to see a goody-goody person? They put onto the stage a goody-goody person. Was there a bad reaction to that? If so, they take it back and put out another facsimile and see how people like that one. Is this facsimile not good enough? Well, here is another. Then they complain about insincere relationships.

Don't put out facsimiles anymore. Put yourself out there. Then if you behave badly and suffer, at least you learn from your experience and take responsibility for it.

28. Miracles are everyday

A FRIEND ASKED ME if I believed in miracles, and I said yes, I believe the whole thing is a miracle. The most miraculous thing about miracles is that they don't seem like miracles.

It is possible, through meditation and spiritual development, to overcome the need for food, sleep or heat. Anyone can accomplish this; it isn't even spectacular.

When one of my sons was in a Benedictine monastery, I visited and met a priest there. It struck me that it was unusual for him to be there. I talked to him and found out he had been an Episcopalian. In World War II he had been on a munitions ship in the China Sea. His ship was hit. He and his mates jumped overboard and were in the water a good distance away when the ship finally exploded.

Because they were in the dark of the moon, no one could see or hear them in the water. So he and his friends joined hands and prayed. As they did, the sky lit up. The light did not come from flares or any other distinguishable source, yet everthing around became visible and they were rescued. To him it was a profound experience, and he became Catholic so he could devote his life to God in a monastery.

Later I asked him how God removes our doubts, and he replied, "He doesn't. That is something we must do ourselves."

The miracle, really, is that we are here.

The miracles in your life will occur when your love of God guides you.

MY OWN ATTITUDE is: What good does it do if you can walk on water? First learn to get through the day. Pay attention to whatever is before you, and do it as well as you possibly can. What matters is your daily life — thinking, doing, serving. The unusual events will come, if necessary, as signposts of your development. They are not the goal. Meditate for peace and love in your life, not for power. These will be the miracles, the power.

29. Be grateful

If you can overcome all these preoccupations of your fantasies and melodramas and your regret about yesterday and your worry about tomorrow, and simply say to God in gratitude, "Thank you, thank you, thank you" for whatever — for another day, for friends, for a job, children — it is as though the scales will fall from your eyes, and you will see the beauty of the world.

DAILY EXPOSURE TO AN UNHAPPY person is a charac-ter-building experience. Gradually you can see how the person's unhappiness comes from a lack of gratitude and awareness.

Where there is no recognition of others there is no recognition of self.

With no gratitude and no awareness of the moment, the life is wasted.

30. Stay in the moment

I AM ALWAYS AMAZED at how clearly people recall unhappy events of the past. It is so much better to be completely in the moment. There is nothing to be done about the past except to learn from it. If people have behaved badly, forget about it. Accept that they were doing their best and avoid them in the future. Do not continue to be with people who have made you unhappy. What can be gained?

The future can only come out of the day. If you do all you can, the future is bound to be better. Anyway, that's all you can do.

31. To have more, want less

LIFE APPEARS BACKWARDS. What we think of as unreal is Real, and the visible reality is unreal. By the same token, some aspects of life work backwards. The way to have more is to want less. The more we give up the more we have.

Giving up does not mean sackcloth and ashes. It just means to empty the mind. See, the mind is full of "People should not wear clothes like that," or "People should not do that." Give up petty judgments and petty desires and simply enjoy what you have.

32. Keep learning

WHEN WE STUDY anything, we learn more about ourselves. We gradually change our behavior and our attitudes. This is part of learning. This is why, when people are unhappy, if they can take up some kind of study, they will see an improvement in their lives. As their behavior changes, everything changes. This can improve the health, brighten the mind and be highly beneficial.

33. Do the divine duty before you

DOING WHAT NEEDS TO BE DONE in our own life as well as we can makes life better. Too often we don't want to do what needs to be done in *our* life.

One woman told me, "I would like to do God's will, but I just don't know what God wants me to do." I told her there is no mystery here. If you have dirty dishes in the sink, God wants you to do the dishes. It's what needs doing. It's just as important to do the dishes as it is to write a poem or sing a song.

If you say, "Well, this doesn't matter, and this does," and "I like this but I don't like that," you are not living in God's world; you are living in your world. In God's world it is all the same — the president or the homeless, everyone has one vote.

Dear Saint Francis was hoeing his garden, and one of his disciples asked him, "Master, if you knew you would die at vespers, what would you do?" Saint Francis replied, "I would finish hoeing my garden."

Techniques for Strength

1. Learn to be artists in religion

WE MUST LEARN to be artists in religion. No reasonable artist says his is the only work of beauty, or that he cannot appreciate the work of others.

All great world religions, at their source, involve themselves with the same basic truths. If you want the discipline of a formal religious sect, the most appropriate one for you is the one you can accept without resistance, so that it is a loving acceptance.

I think it is important to remember, though, that each religion is like a little pitcher. The water in the pitcher comes from the ocean of God. Concentrate on the water. Don't get hung up on the shape of the pitcher.

IT AMAZES ME that so many people seem to think their individual way is The Only Way. This allows everyone to behave in ways that do not seem especially moral or kind. However, as people come to recognize spiritual truths, their behavior becomes automatically what people call

good. The behavior changes not because there is great
regard for what other people think. It changes because the
person recognizes that all actions have a lawful consequence. Realization — not just believing — is what trans-
forms behavior.

ALL MAJOR WORLD RELIGIONS are worthwhile and
helpful. Anything carried to extremes can be dangerous. To
concentrate on right activity rather than good and evil
seems a step forward. Right activity harms no one; that is
why it is right activity.

A NEIGHBOR who treats me as if I were retarded once
said, "Oh, Liz, you are a religious fanatic." When she said
it I knew she had been called a religious fanatic herself and
it hurt her, but I just laughed. I thought it was really funny.
I still do. Religion is not an area I take seriously. The
spiritual path is a different matter. That is why I enjoyed
The Satanic Verses. Salman Rushdie is a wonderful writer;
bitter, but witty and true. Faith that cannot endure ridicule
is not faith.

SOME RELIGIOUS TEACHERS carve out followers with
cookie cutters. This method is effective only while there is
a compelling force behind people to believe in the same
closed way. If the compelling force is anything less than the

direct realization of God, the force will fail in time. Similarly, there is a compelling force behind the establishment and operation of factories and many large organizations. When the unifying drive is lost, the factory disappears, first at the spiritual level, then materially. Some churches are crumbling because they have lost the bond between the mystical experiences and the outer reality. In some places, the ritual, rather than being an engine for realization, has become the residue of it.

A discipline imposed from without is not enough.

RELIGION IS A CONVICTION that profoundly alters our behavior. I remember as a child my Catholic friends saying one "must" go to church at least every Sunday. I remember thinking of the serious consequences of not doing that. I remember feeling an exquisite sense of freedom because I was not convinced that church attendance was that necessary.

Now I know the power of ritual in the daily life and appreciate its value; but there is a difference between one following the ritual out of individual conviction and accepting it without question from others.

A close examination of one's daily life shows the value of a sincere religious effort. Thomas Carlyle said he would not give a farthing for a man's religion unless his dog and cat were the better for it.

2. Love God your way

SURELY YOU REALIZE that God is not simply some wise old man, hanging around in some other galaxy. God is the whole thing, the force behind everything, the All, of which we are a spark.

Though God is unmanifest as well as manifest, we approach God through some personal conception. That conception should be a vehicle but should not be considered a limitation.

IF WE WORSHIP GOD as Father, we attract justice into our lives. If we worship God as Mother, we attract mercy. If we worship God as the abstract Source of creative consciousness, we attract wisdom. Jesus worshiped God as Father. Many Catholics, attracted to God as Divine Mother — a conception dear to many Hindus — worship God through the form of Mary.

If you use some more impersonal or psychological term, that term will do so long as you realize that you are part of a universal power.

The conception of God you accept should be one that makes God a reality in daily life. If you worship God, if you love God, if your activities reflect this devotion, then you don't have to worry about what God is made of or how the world is going to end and such. The amazing thing is that the more you do, the more you can do, so your life is constantly expanding.

3. Find freedom in discipline

IT IS MOST HELPFUL if we impose upon ourselves as much purposeful discipline as we can enjoy living with. I don't believe that a discipline that makes people unhappy or causes suffering is beneficial. From my own experience, though, I know that gradually we can submit to a great deal of discipline, and that within that framework, we can find a great deal of freedom.

If you resent a certain discipline that you otherwise think would be good for you, find out why you resent it. It doesn't do any good, for example, to be an angry vegetarian. But if you accept discipline because of the freedom it affords you, many things that you think you could not live without will fall from you. At first, I know, it is like dying. But if you will walk through that darkness, that aloneness, you will emerge into the light.

One useful discipline in life is to eat and go to bed at approximately the same time — not that anyone should be neurotic about it. While these things seem very tedious and constricting, any discipline like this — physical exercise or meditation at certain times of day — will give you more productive time. Your body will also tune itself to these demands, like a clock, and this programming can make the tasks easier.

The more you concentrate on getting the most out of the 24 hours in your day, the more freedom you will have. You can do what you want to do. You are your only limitation. You are not limited physically, mentally, or spiritually, for even apparent deficiencies can be overcome by will and realization.

Inertia and ignorance are our terrible enemies. We can go to the stars. Or we can stay in our little boxes. But we do not have to stay.

The mind
is like those beautiful, wild horses,
Roaming everywhere,
Unfettered, responding to the sun,
To the moonlight,
To infinite desires.

When we gradually realize
It must be controlled,
We become cunning and watchful.
Little by little we give up

Desires, fears and even anxieties.
Slowly, the horses come near.
Service, deep meditation,
Doing what needs to be done
Creates a corral.

The horse comes in.
The gate is shut.
The long hours of training begin.

Years go by.
The horse is obedient and docile
But can never be allowed
To be free
Of the indomitable will
Which has brought it all about.

4. Pray

ONE OF THE FIRST and easiest disciplines of beginners
on the spiritual path is to pray three times a day — at

sunrise, noon and sunset. Noon is important because the sun is directly overhead, the energy is direct, and the sun is visible evidence of God as a source of life for the earth. Sunrise and sunset are beneficial for prayer or meditation, because then we are neither in the dark nor the light.

Prayer is different from meditation. Prayer is talking to God; meditation is scientific concentration on God to experience the Divine's direct response. At least begin by saying your prayers three times a day. If you only say, "Dear God, I love you," or "Thank you, thank you," that is good.

5. Practice the presence of God

IN YOUR MIND, always talk to God, whether you are working, resting or playing.

Anything we hear from any person that makes us feel better is our awareness of God in that person. That is what love is — the awareness of God's joyful oneness.

If you see God in everyone, you will think, "Here God is like this," and "Here God is like that." You will give up criticizing others. Who can criticize God?

As you refine your perceptions, you will become more sensitive to the response of God. You also will gradually give up the ego's pleasures — the pleasure of being superior, the pleasure of knowing more, the pleasure of being seen as wise, for before God we do not know enough. So you must give up judging yourselves against others. In some areas, someone knows more than you; someone knows less. In accepting this, you become humble automatically.

There is no way you can practice the presence of God and be anything but humble. That is the keystone. St. Francis, who always practiced the presence of God, was humble. Yet you know his name.

Your daily life is like a fabric. Concentrate on the idea that God is the main thread, and the other stuff just gets woven in and out.

6. Evaluate your day

Before you go to bed at night, sit in silence and go back over the day. Soon you will see what makes you happy, what fulfills you, and what does not. You will find that, through your own discrimination, your own effort, you can eliminate nine-tenths of the things that do not make you happy.

Sometimes we believe only great changes can make us happy or productive. This is not true. If you will devote just ten minutes at the end of the day, and look back over your day, gradually you will find that through your own decisions you can renew your life. You will see that much of the misery of life does not come from other people; it comes from our own unhappiness with ourselves.

Unhappiness is not spirituality. The soul is full of joy. At first we imitate the soul, then we gradually join with it.

The Higher Self, the immortal part of us, is totally aware. The ego, the small self, is the part of us that latches on to what we see. Unhappiness comes from the discrepancy between the ego and the Self.

7. Use inner problem-solving methods

THINK OF PROBLEMS as problems, not as some kind of grief and suffering dropped on your head. Just realize that the spirit within you is greater than the problems.

A great American physicist was at a New York dinner party where he sat next to a psychic. He mentioned that he had been working on a physics problem for 10 years and had been unable to figure it out. She told him that if he would outline clearly the problem in his mind before he fell asleep, he would get the answer. The third morning after using this technique, he awoke with the answer.

If you really want to know if what I say is true, ask tonight. Ask, and keep asking. You will get the answer in a way you cannot deny or fail to recognize.

If a severe and seemingly unsolvable problem troubles you, think intensely about it for three hours. If you are burdened by an exceptionally painful problem in which your whole life seems caught up, deal with it fully for three days.

Tell God, "Omnipotent Friend, Maker of all of us, I have this pain I can no longer deal with. You are the ultimate resource. I give it to you." Then meditate and in the calmness that follows, make your decision if a decision is called for. Stick with what feels right at that calm moment.

When you give a problem to God, know that you are giving it to the Creator of the universe. Whenever the worry comes to your mind, say, "I have given it to God." You must do what you can do, but what is beyond you, give to God. Don't keep gnawing, gnawing at yourself.

You have taken care of your part. You are done with it.

If it helps you to concentrate at first, you might light a candle and offer a prayer with that. The candle flame represents the single eye seen deep in meditation when we learn to reverse our energies to begin to perceive the inner forces. The activity of lighting a candle becomes a physical act joined with the mental act. Perhaps the act of lighting the candle and praying will intensify the prayer.

I don't usually speak of too many of these methods to people unless I know them, for I realize that it may seem like black magic or whatever.

As you may know from the various scriptures, there are many things that are very powerful: talismans, symbols, inscriptions, sounds.

There is incredible power available to anyone. No one in his right mind would give even a shred of it to another without some confidence in how the recipient would use that knowledge. It should be enough to realize that the greatest power is love.

Q: What makes the techniques work?

A: We are energy. We can learn to use energy to concentrate on our spiritual growth and solve our problems. Techniques can concentrate our energies. Our thoughts are energy and, through focus and will power, are directors of energy. If we think of a person and concentrate the energy in a particular way, the person can be aware of the thought. This is power.

Another power is intervention. When something is going to happen to a person, something locked into their pattern of living and that can be very destructive, we can intervene to the extent that, even if the blow comes, the blow can be cushioned.

Q: You can do that?

A: Anyone can do that. Prayer is a powerful technique. These things are not in some tiny, secret package that only some people have and nobody else can share. Everything is around all of us always. That is why I tell you to be discriminating about what you think.

Q: Do these techniques come from the East?

A: We all take our little pitcher of water from the same ocean. Don't let anything divide you.

Q: So if you go to church —

A: To a church, temple, tabernacle, mosque — these are a means to an end. Wherever a group thinks of God, the blessing of that thought can sustain you and sanctify that place. But if it takes a seashore to make you think of God, go to the seashore. It is more important to think

God, God, God. Life is not church. Life is school. The church is a school where we should experience results. What we have to learn is the reality of God in us.

8. Repeat an affirmation

THERE ARE QUICK WAYS to control the mind. One is the repetition of a mantra, which is a holy sound. Aum, or what in the Judeo-Christian tradition is written as Amen, and in Islam is spelled Amin, is one verbal attempt at imitating the sound of the vibration upholding creation.

An affirmation helps lift the mind. The affirmation could be frequent mental repetition of a truth such as, "God is the source of all," or a scriptural verse that means a lot to you.

An affirmation lifts the level of your consciousness and can crowd out the more debilitating thoughts and disturbing habits entrenched in the subconscious mind. Habits can be hard to dislodge. The trick to self-mastery is to superimpose better habits; these dominate the lesser habits.

The challenge of living is to extend your consciousness without extending your tendency to pain. All pain is a form of self-indulgence.

To accomplish this, you must control your mind so that you become free from habits and impulses. In linking your will to divine will, you have freedom.

If you have a dog or cat, you train it so it won't mess up your house and run wild. The mind is the same way. The mind runs wild unless it is trained. We talk to ourselves constantly and worry over petty things, argue with ourselves, fantasize uselessly. This talk with the ego keeps the ego active. Control and freedom require that we still the ego.

A repeated spiritual thought or wish can link the conscious, subconscious and superconscious levels of your mind; the unity empowers the wish. That is why it is important for Catholics to say, "Hail Mary" repeatedly with devotion. American Indians used some sounds in chants to bring rain.

Because sound has power at different levels, be careful what you say and think.

In a blizzard with my youngest son, I drove onto a bridge that was iced. The car started careening absolutely out of control. I said, "God, God, God" and instantly, as though hands had grabbed the car, we went straight. Many of us use this power automatically under stress. A greater benefit comes by using mental affirmations.

Similarly, some religions use chants, because the repeated thought drives deeper into the mind. It helps if you realize that our energies go flying in all directions; chants and affirmations help point all the little energies in the same direction. The more we can unify ourselves with the force of life, the more direction and strength we have.

This may seem hard to believe. Proof is not in intellectualizing but in doing. Sound is vibration. The laws of vibration are as natural as the physical laws and gravitational energies that make the sun rise in the east and set in the west. However, if you want to believe the sun is a god in a chariot or whatever, that notion is not going to interfere with the sun. The sun will still come up.

The universe does not depend upon our believing in it.

9. Use symbols

JUST AS THERE ARE basic sounds that can make you happy or sad, so there are symbols that affect you. All religions use symbols.

Symbols often represent patterns of energy. The power of certain symbols is that they can activate certain energies within you automatically. Even squares, circles and triangles have an importance beyond geometry.

Therefore it can be helpful to you to concentrate on religious symbols that attract or have spiritual significance to you — the cross or Star of David, for example, thinking of its meaning.

Also helpful is devotional concentration on the likeness of a spiritual person.

Most of us are caught in a web of emotions, reactions and memories. They can be triggered by scents, songs, scenes and similar reminders. Some people study these activators and use them in advertisements to manipulate us. So you should be discriminating about what you expose yourself to. Do you want television commercials to mold you? Magazine ads? Go to your own heart. Not through a beer jingle. Not through sinus spray. Go through your own control and your own divine perception.

10. Meditate

ANY OF THE THINGS I mentioned will help transform your life. If you ask for guidance, you will get it.

But if you fervently want to know God and complete freedom, you should meditate regularly.

The purpose of meditation, as taught by a true master, is to have such control that you can shut out all your physical senses and enter, with expanded consciousness, into what is called the "second birth" of Spirit. You can see the light of God, hear the Word — the Amen — and become one the great bliss and infinitude of God.

You owe that discovery to yourself. You must ask for the teaching that satisfies you wholly, then use it to make your inner search.

The miracle of the realization of God is that, in a world where everything grows old or falls apart or fails to live up to the warranty, this is the one thing you can depend on. It is the only thing you can depend on.

Mistaken

You have mistaken
Me.
You thought
I was love,
But I am really
Hunger.
And this
Is my companion
Gratification.

The latter
Touched me
Gently
In farewell,
Saying,
Don't feel
Bad.

We are

Often

Mistaken

For

Those others.

I promise you

Q: Liz, could you tell us about some of your earliest, most unusual experiences and generally how you came to the place you are now?

A: My first real experience came when I was two and a half and I realized I was on the earth and did not want to be here. As a baby, I thought of myself as an old man, and being on earth was a severe disappointment. So I was dreadfully ill for a year and sickly afterward until at six I decided to shape up. When I moved to Cleveland as a child with my mother and stepfather, I would tell my brother things I saw and knew, and what I felt. He told me if I kept talking like that, they would just put me away.

Q: Saw things such as what?

A: The spirits in nature. We lived in Lakewood, Ohio, and I understood, through this inner communication, that an oak forest had been slashed down in a very indifferent, even savage way, and the residue of that pain was there. I told my brother how unfortunate it was that the cutters had not even acknowledged the trees in any way.

Though trees obviously do not have brains, all things are composed of intelligent energy and so are aware at a certain level. You can cut down a tree but it is good to tell it so, to acknowledge its existence. That is why you should acknowledge the life around you, touch the plants and trees. Otherwise it is as if you were in a house with people you never speak to. We have a very symbiotic relationship with everything. God is in everything.

When we come to sense our oneness, we are absolved from the need to possess. We don't feel separate. We no longer have to have this or that. We don't have the frantic feeling of being deprived.

When a community is aware, it generates an uplifting, freeing energy. When that energy fragments, the community collapses, then people become obsessed with their own separate careers and survival. That has happened in this nation.

Psychiatrists and psychologists have become our priests. (Priests are people who help us to live.)

As a child, when my cat was healed through prayer in the Christian Science Sunday School, I realized there were enormous energies that people could use, but people were embarrassed to hear or talk about this. So I would just go ahead and use the energies but not talk about them. Any person can do it.

When I was about 12, I realized most people didn't have the experiences I had — knowing what would happen to others, knowing they would soon die or suffer a particular difficulty, so I tried not to know.

Q: What did you do when you could see that someone, say, would die?

A: I just tried to make the moments pleasant. I met many people and knew they would not return from the First World War. At that time I didn't study much or do much. I was like one of those water bugs on top of the water, not really connecting. I gave the appearance of living, superficial but pleasant. Then came the Great Depression, which was a dreary time — precarious but not hopeless — and I tried to shut out the impressions. Sometimes, though, one or two would slip through.

Then I married Bob in 1934. That was sobering. Before that, I had been fanciful and had lived primarily in my mind, though I had friends. I had always understood reality but never really wanted to deal with it. In bringing up my four children I learned that one could make oneself happy most of the time. I doubt that is different for anyone else, but happiness depends on what we can endure and do and the disciplines we follow to make us more aware. Gradually I learned to develop unity between what I believed and what I did. Then came the spiritual path, and I had to get down to the real nitty-gritty. I thought years ago that, if you tried to follow the spiritual path, you would get support from people, but that is not always true. If you try to follow the spiritual path, you will find a great deal of antagonistic energy turned toward you. This is simply a way of finding out if you really want to follow through. If you ignore this, if you cling to the idea that it is better to find God than even to have pleasant surroundings or be with people who are benign, if you cling to the idea of God, God, God no matter what, gradually your surroundings will become more pleasant. This I know from my own experience, and I have seen it in the lives of other people who have undertaken the life of spiritual endeavor. Then — and this is another of those paradoxes — one of the surest signs that you are on the path is that your life becomes easier.

That which is not part of our sense of reality and part of God will fall from us. During World War II some planes were downed in the Arctic. The men set out with all their possessions and artifacts — pictures, mementos and whatnot. By the time they were rescued, they were just in their flying suits. The path behind them was strewn with the things they had let fall. This is the way we walk. We give up our prejudices, our dreams, our illusions.

The difficulty of spiritual advancement is that we have an idea of how the world is. That view feels comforting to us, just as a child feels comfortable in a familiar room. The beginning of the spiritual path is where you have to be courageous. I know, because I've been there.

It is like walking to the edge of the Grand Canyon and saying, "Well, God's going to have to take care of me," and you jump over. All you have is the realization that God will take care of you. After a while you get used to falling. Then you can really see, can be happy, can be loving, but your sense of reality, direction and timing are irrevocably altered.

It is true, as Jesus said, that birds have nests, foxes have lairs, but the Son of Man has nowhere to lay his head.

It gratified me a great deal to read that Dr. Albert Einstein didn't really believe that he, as a physical being, existed, and that he thought there was one great intelligence behind all creation. This is true. You don't exist fundamentally as a physical being. You are an immortal spirit. The whole thing you see is an illusion. Once you realize this, you anchor yourself to the total reality.

You have to jump, yourself. This is what Jesus meant when he said, "If you believe." But he also blessed those who did not believe. So you are blessed no matter where you are. God is in all of us.

One story about the Buddha tells of a woman who had nothing and was taken into a family. She bore a son, and they honored her and gave her food and treated her very kindly. She had never been treated kindly before; it was so wonderful for her. Then the child died. She rushed to the Buddha with the child and pleaded, "Master, Master, restore him." He said, "Bring me a handful of mustard seed from a home in which there has been no death." So she went from house to house, but there was no place that had not seen death. She came to realize that death was part of life. She took the child to the cremation grounds, returned to the Buddha, and said, "I am thine."

It is sad when we must come to God by losing everything. It is much better if you can do it now. Don't wait. A special blessing comes if you turn to God when you are still happy. There is no security in this life; there is only God.

Q: When you were young and recognized the healing energies, how did you use them?

A: The same way you can use them: by directing them with the mind, the will, realization. Realization — just knowing someone will be healed — is the directing force.

Q: What if you can't get it to work?

A: It always works if the person has an illness that is really only relevant to that person. Sometimes people have an illness that affects many people. Many people have to learn or cope by caring for the particular person's illness. For that circumstance there is no cure, but your effort to heal can make the pain less.

Much of what affects us is invisible. There are great energies within us and without. Some can be used; others must be endured.

Energies are thrust through space and go through us like a sieve. The theory of astrology is that rotating matter throws off energy that penetrates our atmosphere and physical bodies. Sometimes energies meet and catch in a pattern. The patterns can cause stress. The stress can manifest in rashes of public behavior — rebellions, assassinations and so on, outward evidence of inward stress, affecting individual and group energy patterns. Sometimes there is little we can do about it except keep our balance and inner peace.

Sometimes we are acting of our own free will. At other times we are responding to those energies. People live in a very closed context, and what may seem whim or chance is locked. We are integral parts of the universe. This should teach us not to impose ourselves on others.

Q: You mean those thrusts of energy can cause wars?

A: The larger energies can combine to intensify individual energies. The effect it has depends on the people's awareness. Out of awareness can come control.

Energies are like germs in an epidemic. The susceptible are affected. The strong may be spared.

Just as individuals have energy patterns, so do groups.

The time to stop wars is when people who fight them are small or unborn. We must practice something in our lives that will affect our daily activities and make peace possible, so that peace is not a reaction but an awareness. We have to get to the place where we move purposefully and not merely react to the things around us. Nations have to learn the same lessons.

We can prevent world destruction, not by refusing to build armaments but by concentrating on the realization that it is all one. The late Hubert Humphrey said we should not spend our time worrying about the future, but should labor every day to make it better.

If you fall into the delusion that we are separate, you will also fall into the delusion that we live only in a little village or state, that we are part of just one country. Dear friends, we have lived in many countries; we have been all races. From here to the end of the universe, we are one.

Remember that nations have the traits of their people's beliefs, acts and histories, and carry the beauty of their enlightenment and the pain of their misconceptions. If you think of yourself as an American or a Russian or a Nigerian, you partake of the risks of whatever you identify yourself with. Love your country, but love all nations with that love. Serve, but disengage yourself from limitations.

Q: Some science-of-the-mind groups say a person has no limitations.

A: Humankind, however, is not the center of the universe. God is the center of the universe. Beware of the teaching of any ritual of self-consciousness that can lead to self-righteousness, which is destructive.

Similarly, don't be egotistical about any spiritual progress you make. When you know enough about driving rules to drive on the correct side of the road, you don't say, "I'm so virtuous and noble for driving down the right-hand side of the road." You drive on the right-hand side of the road because you realize that otherwise you could get killed.

Q: Some people are frightened by the idea of extrasensory perception or seeing ghosts or entities.

A: Reality is more phenomenal than most people admit. There are indeed entities. You are an entity. When you die, you will be an entity at another rate of vibration.

My objection to some horror stories, though, is that they give people the illusion that evil is something separate. Evil is energy directed away from God. Evil is not something that has to overcome us from the outside. I am less frightened by the idea of ghosts or possession than by the fact that Adolf Hitler could think that he was a good man helping his country.

The consciousness of other people affects us. Therefore we should choose what we think about and with whom we associate.

Because of the entertainment, the literature and the times, many people think that if they are not having sexual excitement or drugs or alcohol or something like that, they are not living. These are the delusions of our era. Each era has its own delusions.

It is only fair to tell you that we are coming to a time that will be very difficult. We can all get through it. Realize that any human has infinite resources.

For many years I felt hopeless about the state of the world and what I could see. I did not see how we could be saved. Now I feel differently.

If there are enough of us who believe, who ask for the light of God; if there are enough of us who pray with faith, we still might go through a difficult period, but it will not be as devastating as it could be otherwise.

Remember that even out of catastrophes we can make our blessings. From war, surgical advances have emerged. From local disasters, communities have united to help each other. Perhaps that is Divine Mother's way of compensating us for some of the agonies we bring upon ourselves.

The future will take care of itself if we take care of the present.

Q: Is the United States headed for great change?

A: Yes. Materialism cannot be an end in itself. This country must help lead the world in a spiritual revolution.

Q: Shouldn't other countries as well?

A: They should, but this is a terrible obligation that has been laid upon us. We cannot escape it.

Q: Why?

A: I don't know.

Just love God and do your part. See everyone as one. Go with faith and assurance. We are all just passing through a dream of time. Trust God. Do your best.

You know, one of my dearest friends was 78, and she gave me a wonderful gift: She made me realize that it can be marvelous to grow old. Age gives you freedom. I learned from her that finally you could say whatever you thought, that you could do as you pleased, because there is no one over you who has to be satisfied. It is really rather exciting. You will have a wonderful time when you get old. It is much better to go into the future with that attitude than to fear anything.

Q: Why is it that tonight I have a harder time understanding you than before?

A: We have covered a lot, and tonight you are listening. You'll get it. It will all be clear.

Years ago I studied art with Robert Metcalf. He was such a marvelous teacher. The minute he came into the room and shut the door he started pouring his heart out. Three weeks passed before I knew what he was talking about. I had to learn the language of art, but I listened. To this day — this was more than 20 years ago — when I paint, I hear his voice. And I paint and remember. The information goes to a place. You don't have to think about it. It will be there. Whenever you need it, the information comes back. We really are very intricate beings and have enormous resources.

Remember that the spiritual path — I promise you — is the most exciting thing in the world, the most fulfilling adventure in the world. But you think, "Oh, oh, oh — if I go in there, I will have to give up this and that and, small pleasures that they are, I know them." I promise you —

Open the door.

You all have to open the door.

Jesus says, "Knock, and it will be opened. Ask, and you shall receive." All other great masters say the same.

There is no way that a person can give you spiritual enlightenment. If you ask for it, yes, then you can get it. But nobody can come up to you and say, "Today's the day you are going to have spiritual enlightenment. I'm going to give it to you now."

It's impossible, because it works on a traction. Only when we open our hearts can everything flow.

Realize God as the source of all. Not the economy. Not the job. Not food. Not people. Nothing else; only God. Everything comes from God, the inexhaustible Source.

It is only when we do not see life that we are caught up in it. When we can get any kind of perspective, we can alter life.

Never be discouraged.

Never be lonely.

Wherever you are, love the people you are with; love where you are.

And do your best.

I love you all.